DATE DUE

7/09/13			

Printed
in USA

HIGHSMITH #45230

CHARACTER
IS THE
ISSUE

CHARACTER *IS* THE ISSUE

How

People with Integrity

Can

Revolutionize

America

THE HONORABLE

MIKE HUCKABEE

G o v e r n o r   o f   A r k a n s a s

with John Perry

BROADMAN
&HOLMAN
PUBLISHERS

Nashville, Tennessee

4263-67
0-8054-6367-4

Dewey Decimal Classification: 170
Subject Heading: WHITEWATER SCANDAL / POLITICAL ETHICS
Library of Congress Card Catalog Number: 97-30736

Unless otherwise stated all Scripture citations are from the
New King James Version, © 1979, 1980, 1982,
Thomas Nelson, Inc., Publishers.

Library of Congress Cataloging-in-Publication Data
Huckabee, Mike, 1955–
    Character is the issue : how people with integrity can
revolutionize America
        p.   cm.
    ISBN 0-8054-6367-4
    1. Political ethics—United States. 2. United States—Moral
conditions. 3. Huckabee, Mike, 1955–. 4. Arkansas—Politics and
government—1951– I. Title.
    JK468.E7H831997
    320.973—dc21
                                                        97-30736
                                                        CIP

1 2 3 4 501 00 99 98 97

★ ★ ★

Table of Contents

I n t r o d u c t i o n

Responding to questions regarding his personal character, President Bill Clinton once told his audience that "character isn't the issue." Yet our character defines the world we live in. Our government, welfare programs, schools, and everything else in our lives are shaped and directed according to our character. It's commonly claimed that "you can't legislate morality," but in fact every law in the country is a reflection of our moral values. We have laws against murder and stealing because we believe they are morally wrong. We used to have laws against abortion under most circumstances. When our moral values changed, the laws changed along with them.

Over the past thirty years, a decline in moral character has produced a decline in the character of our society. Columnists and researchers have produced a whole library of books and reports on the issue and laid blame for our cultural troubles on everything from government policy to single parent households. What it all comes down to, though, is that people of good, godly character make good, godly laws. Everything hinges on the character of the men and women we choose to establish public policies.

And their character depends on you.

This is a book for everyone who looks out at the world, sees the moral decline that seems to be devouring our culture unchecked, and thinks, *Our country is falling apart and there's nothing I can do about it.*

There *is* something you can do about it: you can live a God-centered life of high moral character, and you can run for public office or support candidates who share your Christian standards. At first that sounds like an oversimplification—maybe even an impossibility—but I can tell you from personal experience that it can happen.

Seven years ago I was the pastor of a wonderful church in Texarkana, Arkansas. We had a growing church, an active television ministry, and a wide-ranging series of community outreach programs. But I felt God's call to leave the pulpit and take my message into the political arena. I had no experience in politics. I was a Republican in a heavily Democratic state. And yet I had a God-centered worldview that my fellow Arkansans identified with.

My views didn't make me any better than anyone else before God, but they struck a chord with people who were weary of living under a government that no longer respected what they thought was important. Today as governor of Arkansas, I recognize the same moral authority—God's authority—that I did as a pastor, as a student, and as a radio disc jockey in high school.

God's standards never change; they are an unmoving goal toward which we can travel all our lives without ever having to change direction.

There are three sections in this book, each dealing with a different aspect of how character shapes the events and institutions of our culture. The first section gives examples of how character can direct the outcome of a crisis. From political showdowns to life-threatening illness, character equips us to face daunting challenges and prevail over them.

The second section focuses on why character is important, how we know there are absolutes of good and bad character, and the consequences of surrendering those absolutes to the champions of relativism.

The final section, composed of speeches and public commentary, shows how character decisions translate directly into public policy decisions.

Character is the issue, and your character makes a difference every day—in the work you do, the candidates you vote for, the people who look to you for leadership. My hope is that this book will encourage you to live your faith proudly and publicly, and to support and uplift fellow Christians as we work together to build God's kingdom.

Part I

★ ★ ★

CHARACTER IN THE FURNACE

★ ★ ★

I

* * *

A   C r u c i b l e   M o m e n t

My office wasn't the best place in the world to rehearse a speech, but my staff was doing its best to keep interruptions to a minimum. Outside the door, people were running around like members of a pit crew working the Indianapolis 500—fast, efficient, focused, everybody with a job to do, swarming everywhere at once.

It was 1:40 P.M. I wasn't going on the air for several hours, but this was my only opportunity to practice my speech from the TelePrompTer. In twenty minutes I was scheduled to be sworn in as governor of Arkansas. Meetings and other official duties would follow, right up to the time of my live, statewide address at 5:15 P.M.

I had spent days writing and timing this speech; I wanted to make sure everything was just right. (See appendix 1.)

In the relative calm of the capitol office which I had used for almost three years as lieutenant governor, I sat at my desk and read aloud:

> . . . The responsibility that has been thrust upon me and entrusted to me is one that I approach with unapologetic dependence upon the Spirit of God to give me the heart of a servant, wisdom for the difficult decisions I will face each day, the courage to stand by my convictions, and the humility to acknowledge my mistakes, of which there will be many.
>
> A few weeks ago, when a jury of our fellow Arkansans patiently reached a verdict in a nearby federal courthouse, our state was shattered emotionally and politically. My decision to withdraw from the race for the United States Senate and concentrate wholeheartedly on serving you as governor is one I do not regret. I want to help restore Arkansas's image to America as a place of natural beauty, hard-working people, and a family-friendly atmosphere. . . .

Less than two months before, on May 28, 1996, Governor Jim Guy Tucker had been convicted on federal charges of fraud and conspiracy in the first Whitewater trial. Jim and Susan McDougal, principals in Madison Guaranty Savings and Loan, had been convicted the same day. While the McDougals had gotten more national publicity because of their ties to Governor

Tucker's predecessor in office, President Bill Clinton, Tucker's conviction had a far greater effect on the people of Arkansas.

After his conviction was announced, Governor Tucker made a promise to the people of Arkansas that he would resign as governor on or before July 15, 1996. That meant I would move into the governor's office, becoming only the third Republican governor since Reconstruction. At the time, I had a double-digit lead in the race for a seat vacated by popular Democrat David Pryor in the United States Senate but had pulled out of the campaign to concentrate my energies on my duties as governor. Arkansas remained one of the few states whose people had never elected a Republican senator, and if I were to be elected it would be political history. As it turned out, an even more historic moment was about to occur.

As I continued practicing my speech, friends and staff members walked in and out of the office, some of them talking quietly in a far corner of the room. Monday, July 15, was a brutally hot day in Little Rock. With a dozen people or more in the office, it was getting stuffy despite the air conditioning.

Nearing the end of my script, I looked into the Tele-PrompTer and read: "Being governor of Arkansas is an honor I could never have imagined as a small boy growing up under modest circumstances. I only wish my father could have lived just four more months to have witnessed this day. But somehow, I can't help but believe he's watching all of it from the best seat in the house. When I was fifteen years old, a verse from the New Testament, Philippians 4:13, changed my life. It says, 'I can do all things through Christ who strengthens me.' I'll do my best.

And with my family's support, your prayers, and God's help, I can do this job. . . ."

It was 1:55 P.M. The speech timed out perfectly. (Stopwatches held by staff members Gary Underwood and Rex Nelson were within two seconds of fifteen minutes.) Any moment now, a delegation from the state legislature, already in session at the other end of the capitol, would arrive to provide the traditional escort for the governor-elect through the marble corridors and into the House chamber. The official swearing-in would be at 2:00 P.M., followed by a public ceremony and rally outside on the capitol steps an hour later.

★ ★ ★

A Disturbing Surprise

I was stretching my legs and talking to Rex, my new communications director, when the phone rang. It was Dawn Cook, my personal secretary, who would be moving with me down the hall into the governor's office. She said Governor Tucker was on the line. I thought he was making a courtesy call to tell me the keys were in the desk and to wish me well. The transition had not been easy, and I was relieved that at this late moment he would have a word of advice or encouragement.

"Hello, Governor," I said when he came on the line. I signaled for quiet in the room and the rumble of conversation stopped.

"Hello, Mike," Tucker began. "I hope everything went OK out at the church."

That morning there had been a prayer and dedication service at First Baptist Church of Little Rock. Some of my pastor friends from my years as a Baptist minister were there, and each one read Scripture, or gave a sermon or a charge. Stirring music filled the sanctuary. It was almost like an ordination service, as if every person who spoke made statements that prepared us for the unexpected events of the rest of the day. I will always believe that service was the turning point for me in preparing for a challenge I could never have imagined.

"Yes, it was a very nice service," I responded, thinking that his question seemed odd under the circumstances.

"I'm glad everything went well." He was stalling. Something was up.

After a few seconds of awkward silence, he continued. "Well, I wanted to let you know I've decided not to resign. I filed a motion to appeal on Friday, and until the court rules on it, I feel I should continue in office. I'm going to declare disability and let you serve as acting governor until then. At that time I can make some final disposition."

Not resigning! They were the most unbelievable words I'd ever heard. I signaled for a piece of paper. This was a historic conversation, and I wanted to record both sides of it. Somebody handed me a yellow pad, and I started scribbling as fast as I could. Rex looked at my first words at the top of the page: "Not Resigning!"

To the rest of the people in the room, Rex mouthed silently, "He's not resigning."

I scribbled as Governor Tucker talked. "If my appeal is granted and the verdict is overturned," he told me, "it would be unfair to the people who elected me for me to give up my office."

Brenda Turner, our chief of staff, looked at me with eyes as big as dinner plates. There had been no warning of this. Neither the legislature nor my office had been notified that the governor had changed his mind.

"Governor," I answered, "I'm supposed to take the oath of office in five minutes. The legislative escort is probably waiting outside my door. I respectfully ask that you reconsider this action, not only to keep your word, but for the welfare of the state of Arkansas."

"The people of Arkansas voted for me," he said. "Over four hundred thousand of them elected me governor. They didn't elect you."

This was simply bizarre. He was totally out of touch with reality. I knew a confrontation would be useless, so I tried to steer the conversation toward his place in history and the importance of acting for the good of the state.

"I don't think the people of Arkansas will understand," I told him. "You didn't place any conditions or limitations on your promise to resign, and to go back on that now would very likely be seen as a breach of public trust. Governor, I think that you need to reconsider. The people of Arkansas will think you're going back on your word."

By this time hundreds of spectators had gathered for the ceremony, many of whom had taken a vacation day to be present. A full afternoon and evening of activities had been planned. As we spoke, my staff was moving into the governor's office down the hall while Tucker's was moving out. Mine had quit other jobs to join me; many of his staff had lined up new positions and already had made commitments to new employers.

"Governor," I said, "we have people who have left their jobs and sold their homes who are on the job today. And, as you know, members of your staff have moved and have taken other jobs."

"Well, I realize that is going to be a problem," he agreed, "but that's just something that we'll have to work through. Now as far as you're concerned, you can go ahead and move into the governor's mansion. You'll have full use of the house and security staff, and you'll have the salary. And if I need to come back, we will just deal with that."

I couldn't imagine anything more impractical. It was a crazy idea. "Governor," I said, "do you honestly expect me to move my family a hundred and fifty miles up here from Texarkana, move my furniture, get my kids enrolled in school, and then have you decide in six weeks you're going to come back? Does that seem reasonable?"

My wife, Janet, walked up beside me and squeezed my arm. When someone's trying to rewrite your life over the telephone, God's gift of a wonderful spouse is truly a blessing to be treasured. Yet nothing I said could change the governor's mind.

"Well, I'll consider what you said and let you know," he said. I hung up the phone.

★   ★   ★

A Crisis Looms

"He's not resigning," I announced to those in the room. During the course of a ten-minute conversation, we had moved from a day of celebration to arguably the greatest constitutional crisis in Arkansas history. "We can't let this happen," I declared. "We have to uphold an orderly transfer of power. We cannot let Governor Tucker go back on his promise; we should move forward. Acceptance of this is not an option. If there's anyone who doesn't agree with me on this, speak now or forever hold your peace."

No one spoke.

I turned to Brenda. "We've got to know what our legal options are. See if you can get Leon Holmes in here. He's the best constitutional lawyer in the state. And Frank Arey. And notify Judge Holt." Frank Arey was my new chief legal counsel, while Jack Holt Jr. was the former chief justice of the Arkansas Supreme Court, a Democrat who had advised us during the transition.

Someone turned on a TV. Live coverage of the ceremony had begun. Pictures of the House chamber filled the screen. State representatives were waiting impatiently, looking at their watches.

It was 2:15 P.M. The legislative escort had been waiting for me about twenty minutes. We told them there had been a short delay and we weren't ready yet. They returned to the legislative chamber empty-handed, knowing something wasn't right, but suspecting we were having trouble ironing out details of the ceremony.

The telephone on my desk rang. The call got cut off somehow, and while the operator was putting it through again, I was handed a letter from the governor. As I opened the envelope, the phone rang a second time. Governor Tucker was on the line. Had I received his letter?

"It was just handed to me. I'm reading it now," I answered.

In the letter he repeated the position he had taken on the phone. He was declaring himself disabled and temporarily "unable to discharge the duties of the Office of Governor," according to provisions in the state constitution. "This decision to declare an inability to serve," the letter read, "arises from the discovery just last week that goes to the heart of my citizen's right to receive a fair trial from an impartial jury."

A member of the Whitewater jury that convicted him, he explained, married a prisoner who had once petitioned the governor to commute his forty-year sentence for cocaine possession. The governor had refused. This, he claimed, had prejudiced the juror against him. "I expect the court to grant a hearing on this issue and decide this matter prior to August 19, 1996. If the verdict is set aside, it eliminates the reason for my decision to resign. . . ."

Now he told me he had been considering our earlier conversation. "I thought this over," he said. "It's clear to me what I should do, and my mind is made up. I'm going to declare disability. I will effectively now turn the controls of government over to you and, after this is resolved in August, I will make a final disposition. I expect that I will be fully exonerated and will resume the duties of governor at that time."

"How will you handle the announcement to the House and Senate, as well as to the public?" I asked.

He had sent the legislature the same note I had received, he said, and he considered that sufficient.

"This can be an easy transition or a hard one," he continued. "It all depends on you." I replied that I respectfully disagreed. That decision was in his court, not mine.

★   ★   ★

The News Spreads

Meanwhile on television, House parliamentarian Tim Massanelli was reading a copy of the governor's letter to a dumbfounded legislature and the hundreds of guests who had crowded into the chamber for the ceremony. The buzz of voices rose steadily as the letter was read. When Mr. Massanelli looked up from the page after reading the last word, the buzz became a roar. The state supreme court justices stood and filed out of the chamber.

Many of the old-time Democrats all but fell on the floor and ripped their garments in twain. It had been bad enough to have a Democratic governor leave office after being convicted on felony charges. But then to have him pull this stunt in a state where honor means so much was almost more than they could bear. Keeping your word is a sacred thing in Arkansas. My dad used to say, "The only thing a poor man has is his word. It's the one thing nobody can take from you." It looked as if our governor had given his away.

Though I didn't know it then, Governor Tucker called a news conference just after our phone conversation. "If I am to resign, there should be a reason," he told the press, assembled in the high-ceilinged governor's conference room. "The elimination of the verdict would eliminate the reason for my announced resignation. I regret if it causes anyone any inconvenience, but I expect this will be as smooth and orderly as those involved wish to make it. I'm sure there will be those who will want to have a fight and disagree about it. If that's what they choose to do, that's how it will have to be."

The governor and his wife, Betty, then left the capitol, surrounded by a protective cordon of state police. Word of his decision had spread to the huge crowd outside. Sight of him prompted an immediate, raw, visceral reaction—people booed, screamed, and shouted, "Liar!" "How could you?" "You're a disgrace!" On reading the newspaper account later, I felt so sorry for this man and his wife. There was no joy, no benefit to anyone, in their tragic decision.

After my second phone conversation with the governor, I looked around at my staff members and friends filling the office. "One man's misjudgment is not going to jeopardize the future of two and a half million Arkansans," I declared. "I want us to move forward with dignity. I want it done right. But on the other hand, this is one of those crucible moments in the history of this state. If we allow this sort of outrageous indifference to promises, to the laws of this state, and to the people of this state, then we are responsible."

"Can you accept legal responsibility for this?" someone asked.

"I don't see how we cannot accept legal responsibility," I answered.

It wasn't a matter of politics or parties or careers. It was a matter of Governor Tucker keeping his oath to the people of Arkansas, and of me keeping mine. If people were determined to think I was going after the governor for my own benefit, so be it.

The legislature and the people had to be reassured that the office of the governor was being safeguarded, that the lines of responsibility and command were clear even in this time of crisis. Reporters wanted to know who was in control of the National Guard. The state police had to know who the governor's security detail was supposed to protect.

I told those in my office that I thought I should address the legislature if the governor would not. Several of them suggested that I wait until my scheduled television address at 5:15 P.M., a little more than two and a half hours away. I thought momentarily of my carefully rehearsed speech—now worthless—and wondered what I would say instead.

"I don't think we should wait that long," I said. "The citizens of Arkansas need to know what's going on. If there's a question we can't answer, we'll be honest and say we don't know." I took the position that I had assumed the responsibilities of governor at noon, the time Tucker had set for his resignation. Until legal counsel or the courts said otherwise, that would be our view.

It was a controversial decision. As discussion continued, more staff members voiced their opposition to my facing the legislature in person. I was thinking, *I can either leave it up to Tucker—because he is the one who has made them angry—or I can go down there and speak to them and try to salvage the situation.*

Finally I said, "I do not want to hide out or crawl under the table. I think I should tell the legislature we can accept this letter and let one person guide our destiny, or we can stand together and explore our options."

Once I made up my mind, I was very firm about my decision. I resolved to go face-to-face with the legislature and take charge. Governor Tucker's actions were unacceptable. His decision-making ability was clearly impaired, and I had to demonstrate to the legislature that we had to stand together and take action for the good of the state. The governor *was* disabled, but not just temporarily. He was incapable of discharging the responsibilities of his office.

Rex went into the hallway to answer what questions he could. Releasing what little information we could would be better than allowing the rumor mill to get cranking.

"Does Governor Huckabee's staff have a budget?" a reporter asked.

"No," Rex replied. "We're all working as volunteers until further notice."

"Who has the powers of office at this moment?"

"Acting Governor Huckabee has been given the powers of office, according to the state constitution. He's meeting with advisors now to look at how best to proceed." Whether those official powers were permanent or temporary remained to be seen.

"What about all the receptions and other activities planned for tonight?"

"They're still on, as scheduled. And Acting Governor Huckabee will still make his statewide address at 5:15."

★ ★ ★

A Humbling Moment

A little before 3:00 P.M., an Arkansas State Police security detail, assisted by Capitol Police officers, escorted Janet, the children (John Mark, 20; David, 16; and Sarah, 13), members of the staff, and me to the House chamber. The security team cleared a path in the hallway outside my office, and we opened the door. The enormous, elegant hall was packed shoulder-to-shoulder with well-wishers who started clapping and cheering, their shouts echoing off the bright white marble walls. All the way up the marble staircase to the House, the crowd lined both balustrades, parting far enough only to let the officers by, with the rest of us following in a compacted clump behind them. Sarah lost her place behind the police and was swallowed up in the crowd. Several people fell back to rescue her. Unable to work their way back to us, they returned to my office to watch the proceedings on television.

As we approached the huge, ornate double doors with "HOUSE" carved in the marble overhead, citizens jamming the stairs and hallway and spilling out onto the sidewalk around the capitol began to chant, "We want Mike! We want Mike! We want *Mike!* We want MIKE!" As soon as the doors to the chamber were opened, an enormous swell of cheers and applause cascaded out, roiling with the noise in the hallway. The commotion was so loud that we couldn't hear the doorkeeper announce us to the Speaker. After a moment, Janet and I walked to our place on the dais through a sea of standing, jumping, exuberant people, some of them waving with both hands.

It was one of the most humbling moments of my life (and as clear an example as I ever expect to see of God's divine providence working in my life). It wasn't my political skills or anything else of my own doing that had brought me to this moment. Only God could have done this.

Bobby Hogue, Speaker of the House, called for order and the turmoil began to subside. My good friend Roy Parker, pastor of Beech Street First Baptist Church, the church I had once pastored in Texarkana, offered a short prayer. After the Pledge of Allegiance, I was introduced as "Lieutenant Governor Mike Hucka-bee, acting governor of the great state of Arkansas." The roar of applause erupted again as I stood and walked to the podium. After a moment it grew quiet enough for me to speak. The atmosphere was electric. Supercharged.

"Is there something going on here this afternoon that I need to know about?" I asked.

As I had hoped, my question broke the tension. Laughter rippled through the auditorium, then silence. I glanced at the single sheet of notes I had hurriedly prepared and went on. I had been tempted to send a written message to the chamber, but decided to speak directly to them. And so I began: "I've chosen to come and speak to you face-to-face and heart-to-heart."

That remark brought more cheers. Though I appreciated the response, I suggested listeners hold their applause, considering the seriousness of the occasion. I recapped the information outlined in the letter we all had just received. "This is a very critical moment in our state's history," I said, "and it demands that our response be measured only by how effectively we as elected officials act with the caliber of calm yet courage required for such a moment in our history. I would like to request an immediate meeting with the Speaker of the House and the president pro tempore of the Senate. . . ."

I added that I would still address the state at 5:15 P.M. and at that time would report on our meeting to all the citizens of the state, including public officials "who, with me, have been elected to stand tall in a moment like this . . . to represent not what we think or what we hope, or believe, but to represent the heart, the mind, and the very essence of the people who put us in these sacred positions of trust."

The chamber roared with applause as Janet and I stepped down from the podium. That was the turning point of the day. I doubt the legislature expected me to exhibit such a clear direction and firm hand. We were calm but resolved. Our team showed a strong focus. Nobody was overly excited, which was amazing. Nobody panicked. We had a job to do, and we were going to do it. It was orderly and methodical.

★   ★   ★

Crucial Steps

A few minutes later we were sitting in my office with Speaker Bobby Hogue and Senate President Pro Tempore Stanley Russ. We had to make important decisions quickly, in a spirit of unity. We couldn't begin with ambivalence.

"Here is the situation," I told them. "What is happening here is completely unacceptable. The people of this state are looking to us for leadership. They need to know their state is under control. What the governor has done is outrageous and unacceptable. It is a betrayal of the public trust, and we have got to make it very clear that this isn't going to work."

Bobby and Stanley were two experienced, capable Democratic legislators in the most lopsidedly Democratic state legislature in the country. I doubt they ever expected to hear words like that from a Republican acting governor.

I said to Bobby, "A lot of people are going to want to blame, not Jim Guy Tucker, but you and the Democratic Party. They're ready to believe this is a conspiracy. I know that's not true. I believe that you are as shocked as I am about what he has done. I believe that this is the act of a single individual and not of the party. I am willing to stand with you publicly to defend your honor with this, but I expect you to stand with me publicly as I take us through these next few hours.

"It is not my intention to hurt Governor Tucker or the Democratic Party. It is simply our goal to move on. Really, his only options are to resign or to have us call for his impeachment. I have a televised address in less than two hours. The time is reserved, and I *will* be talking to the people of Arkansas. You need to talk to Governor Tucker and tell him that if he will resign unconditionally before five o'clock this afternoon, then we will never use the word 'impeachment.' We'll just let it be that he has reconsidered, has resigned as he promised to do, and there will never be any other discussion about it. But if he does not resign by five o'clock, at 5:15 P.M. I will be on the air and I will call for his impeachment. I will announce that we are in the process of preparing the necessary papers, that I am calling the General Assembly into a special session Wednesday for the purpose of beginning impeachment proceedings. He needs to know that I am resolved in this." They agreed to talk with him about it.

I then left for the Excelsior Hotel downtown to change and shave in preparation for the telecast. While there, I got a call from Hogue and Russ with news I didn't want to hear: the governor had no intention of resigning.

II

★ ★ ★

A   D e l i c a t e   V e s s e l

It was time for my television address to be broadcast from my office. A TV crew covered the windows with black paper and set up its lights and cameras. I took my place in a chair in the middle of the room. The TelePrompTer was in position—but revealed only a blank screen. Three and a half hours earlier in the same room, I had rehearsed a speech carefully crafted for the occasion. It seemed like a year ago. And history had sent that script straight to the trash can.

"Thirty seconds to air."

I felt no sense of discomfort or apprehension. I would say what I knew was right for our state, what God had put in my heart.

"Ten seconds and counting. . . . Five seconds. . . . Cue."

> Tonight I stand before you with no script, with
> no written words, just a few moments to share

with you from the depths of my heart as a fellow
Arkansas citizen exactly where we are in this very
critical moment in our state's history. . . . What
really is at issue tonight is a simple question
between right and wrong. This afternoon, I spent
a lot of time listening to legal counsel—wise and
experienced people of the law. There are as many
opinions as there are lawyers, as you know. But as
this hour approached, I realized that this is not
the time for a committee decision. What we have
to do is come to a place where we take clear and
decisive action because, frankly, that is what you
have elected us to do. . . .

I tried very diligently to be cooperative and to
be quiet about the actions of the past seven
weeks—the hundreds of appointments, the nearly
$58 million in state money. [Between the May 28
verdict and July 15, the governor had made more
than three hundred political appointments—
including 174 in a single day!—and spent almost
$58 million.] I remained silent because the gover-
nor was still the governor until a court said he was
not. . . . We never imagined the governor would
make any kind of decision like this. . . .

We received the letters indicating his refusal to
step down. . . . There are many who will probably
say this is going to be great for the Republicans.
My friends, this is simply going to be bad for all
of us. No Republican could ever take pleasure in

what has happened, nor should any Democrat be branded with the responsibility of it. . . .

The governor has been notified that as of nine o'clock in the morning if we have not received from him a letter of unreserved and unqualified resignation, a proclamation which is being prepared even as I speak will be signed and put into motion first thing in the morning. That proclamation will call for an immediate, emergency session of the General Assembly. We will ask the members of the Arkansas House and Senate to convene on Wednesday morning at ten o'clock for the purpose of initiating the process of impeachment and ultimately the removal from office of Jim Guy Tucker as governor of Arkansas. . . .

If there are court challenges, let them come. We're more than ready to face them. If there are challenges from those who write columns or make opinions, let them come. We have not been elected to take a poll or check with opinion writers, or even to be threatened with legal action. We have been elected to serve you and represent you. . . .

Here is what I pledge to you. I'll make my share of mistakes. Always have, always will. That is why I am grateful to God that He is a God who looks at us—with all He knows about us—and still loves us, still forgives us, still empowers us to go on. Now there are those who tell me, "Mike, don't make so many quotes from the Bible in your speeches." Well, a word to those who would per-haps, with good intentions, tell me not to refer-ence God or the Bible. The fact is that since my childhood, that Book and its Author have been the guiding forces in my life. And it would be much easier for me to give up being governor than it would be to give up taking the counsel that I have had from God and His Word.

Now I very much hope and trust that each one of you as Arkansas citizens will let your desires be known to your representative and your state sen-ator. You elected them to represent you, and I believe these are honorable men and women. Don't think that the Democratic representatives don't feel equally embarrassed. Don't think that they have some agenda here other than what is best for Arkansas. Call them. Let them know tonight and tomorrow your feelings and desires. And let us all pray that Governor Tucker will do the right thing for Arkansas, for the Tuckers, and for Arkansas history.

Finally the TV lights went off and somebody took the black paper off the windows. "Nobody will ever believe you didn't have a script," the cameraman said.

Let the words of my mouth . . .

be acceptable in Your sight, O LORD . . . .

Psalm 19:14

After the speech, I learned that State Attorney General Winston Bryant was already setting the legal wheels in motion. He had announced his intention to file suit in circuit court to have Governor Tucker removed from office and was urging lawmakers to consider impeachment.

Bryant was in a tough spot because he faced criticism no matter what he did, whether he supported the governor or opposed him. He was the Democratic nominee for the U.S. Senate race in November and would have run against me had I not dropped out to assume the duties of governor. Nonpartisan polls had me more than fifteen points ahead. If Bryant pressed for Tucker's removal, he would be accused of trying to take out Tucker so I would become governor, drop out of the Senate race, and make it easier for Bryant to win.

Legally, though, there was a big question whether Tucker could remain in office as a convicted felon. Some accused Bryant of being too chummy with the governor and too protective of Democratic Party turf. Tucker's political appointments and runaway spending after May 28 were legally suspect, but Bryant had chosen to leave the issue alone. "Well, we don't really know what we should do," he'd say.

Yet suddenly, on the afternoon of July 15, he declared he was going to file a lawsuit in the morning and challenge the legality of Tucker's remaining in office. Bryant could see that the train was about to leave the station and he wanted to be on board. I've kidded him about it since, but in all fairness, he didn't have a lot of options.

* * *

The Second Letter

After the television address, we set up an impromptu news conference in the hallway outside my office. I had answered only a few questions when Rex came out, interrupted me, and called me back inside. We had just received a second letter from Governor Tucker: "The Republican lieutenant governor has informed me that he intends to call a special session of the General Assembly. I hereby notify you that my inability to serve as governor has ended and I have resumed the powers of the office of governor as of 4:40 P.M., July 15, 1996."

Again, we huddled in my office to discuss our options. The lines of authority could get confused quickly unless we took decisive action. I carried Governor Tucker's two letters to me back into the hallway where the reporters and others were waiting. I read the second letter, in which the governor claimed his inability to serve had ended. Then I read part of the first, where he described his inability to serve as being caused by his felony convictions currently under appeal.

"His inability has not ended," I pointed out. "His appeal is still pending, and he still needs to honor his promise to resign today without qualification."

The second letter reopened the question of exactly who was governor at the moment. Who should the governor's security detail protect? Who commanded the National Guard? My stance was unwavering: "You follow my orders. You have to make a choice, but I am expecting you to follow mine."

At that point everything fell apart for the governor and his allies. The Democratic leadership had done its best to help him work his way out of this mess, but when he tried to reclaim the reins of power, even his closest friends began to distance themselves from him.

All of us, Democrats and Republicans, were pulling together for a common good. We realized that we had to make decisions thoughtfully. We had to do it right because we would have no opportunity to do it over.

Once more I affirmed that I held the duties and responsibilities of governor until a court ruled otherwise. I encouraged everyone to call their state representatives and senators. It would be their decision whether to accept Tucker's demands or vote to begin impeachment proceedings.

I think we all sensed the gravity of the day. The Arkansas Constitution at that moment was a delicate vessel that had been placed in our hands, and we were responsible for seeing that it was not dropped and shattered, but rather that we handed back to the people a stable government that had their full confidence.

News of the crisis had worked its way down the street to the federal building, where the *New York Times* and other national press were covering a Whitewater trial. It was a slow day there, and many of the out-of-state reporters left the federal courthouse to join the Arkansas press corps at the capitol. The whole country would be watching to see how the state and its leaders responded. What would happen?

Even in this crisis, the ultimate decision was in the hands of the citizens. If they insisted on Tucker's return, their representatives in the General Assembly would vote against the resolution to impeach. If they were willing to accept my leadership, they could call their legislators and say so.

Over at the offices of the *Arkansas Democrat-Gazette,* the switchboard lit up like the Fourth of July as citizens called to get the names of their districts' senators and representatives.

The tension of the situation had prompted the head of the state police to station thirty or forty state troopers at the capitol and have another thirty or forty standing by. Everybody they could get into uniform was on duty. Even Jim Clark, who runs the crime lab, was standing guard.

In the hall at the capitol, Speaker Hogue spoke briefly to reporters. He said he had talked with Governor Tucker and that he had stood with him through a lot, but could stand with him no more. He had advised the governor to resign and would support a motion for impeachment on Wednesday. It took a great deal of courage to stand in front of the national press and take sides against a governor of his own party. But as I had said a few minutes before on the air, this was no time for Democrats and Republicans to draw sides; it was a time to draw together.

✶ ✶ ✶

The Crisis Subsides

As I was answering one reporter's question, a radio correspondent holding a cellular phone interrupted me. "Our newsroom is saying they've just gotten word that Tucker has resigned," he announced.

"Governor," Rex quickly interjected, "we best go inside and get some information." I went back into the office to chase down this latest rumor. It didn't take long to uncover the facts.

Tucker had in fact decided to resign. Sharon Priest, the Arkansas secretary of state, had traveled to Democratic Party headquarters to receive his resignation letter. She drove back to the capitol, parked her car, and was climbing the steps. Larry Audas, a news anchor for Channel 11, a Little Rock station broadcasting live, stuck a microphone in her face and said, "Ms. Priest, any new developments?"

"Well," she answered, "I've got this resignation here in my hand from Governor Tucker."

What a scoop!

Larry read the letter on the air, a handwritten note on governor's mansion stationery, addressed to the president pro tempore of the senate. "Dear Mr. President: This is to inform you that I hereby resign the office of governor effective at 6:00 P.M. July 15, 1996."

When word of the resignation reached the reporters and others standing in the hall, a roar of applause thundered through the vast marble area. I don't think it was the sound of political victory because politics weren't the issue. Character was the issue; the resolve to do right, regardless of the circumstances or of the consequences, was the issue. It was the sound of relief, of thanksgiving, of celebration that we had prevailed together in a crisis.

What Jim Guy Tucker had unintentionally done was to give the new administration the emotional mandate of the people. He also gave us the opportunity to show we could handle pressure. It might have taken months or years to prove those things in the course of handling routine state business. But from the first hour, nobody who knew the facts could say we were inept lightweights, caretakers, or lame ducks.

The swearing-in ceremony was rescheduled for 6:45 that evening. Busloads of friends from across the state, who had waited all afternoon to see what would happen, filed back into the House chamber. Speaker Hogue called the session to order, and this time the ceremony went off exactly as planned. With my hand on a green leather Bible, which Janet held, I took the oath of office from the chief justice of the Arkansas Supreme Court. In a few brief remarks, I said again that I hoped no one would see this as an opportunity for gloating or political posturing. It was time to put this sad episode behind us and get on with the business of making Arkansas an even better place to live.

The caterers at the convention center had been keeping vigil, hoping the cakes that said "Congratulations Governor Huckabee" wouldn't end up an embarrassment. The party started a little late, but the cakes fit right in. Finally, I could celebrate and thank all the people who had worked so hard during the seven weeks of transition, supporters who had been so efficient and clearheaded during this long day of crisis.

The day proved to me that when everybody shares the view that *right* and *truth* are not relative conditions, but absolutes, you don't have to spend a lot of time explaining what to do and why. A few clear, immovable milestones made the day's decisions easy. We couldn't let the irrational decisions of one person control the destiny of Arkansas; that would have been wrong. We couldn't worry about the opinion makers and naysayers; if we were resolved to do right, their opinions were irrelevant. We couldn't fret about the political or legal liabilities we might have incurred; they were simply part of the cost of sticking to our moral guns.

Some people don't believe in moral absolutes and the power of integrity. I would challenge them to chart a successful path through a *real* crisis with an untested team using any other standards. I don't think it can be done.

Late that night back at the Excelsior Hotel, where we were to stay until we could occupy the governor's mansion, I kept replaying the events of that historic and bizarre day. How could someone with the political savvy and experience of Jim Guy Tucker do what he had done?

Perhaps the bitterness and resentment he felt as a result of his conviction grew to the point that they got the upper hand. In the end, he had unintentionally done me a favor. On the morning of July 15, plenty of people thought I was an untested, bomb-throwing, right-wing, Christian fundamentalist Republican who would assume a caretaker position until a real governor could be elected. By the end of the day, I felt an overwhelming majority of citizens wanted me to succeed. It had been a long day, and at last it was over.

But the surprises weren't.

III

The People Rule

My first full day as governor got off to a much better start than my first day as lieutenant governor. For one thing, my office door wasn't nailed shut from the inside.

When I had arrived at the capitol as the newly elected lieutenant governor in 1993, the door to my office seemed to be jammed or blocked. I couldn't get it open. It didn't take long to figure out that the door had been nailed shut all the way around the frame from the inside.

"We're going to use the room for the Martin Luther King Jr. Commission," I was told, even though the commission hadn't yet started its work. I couldn't get a straight answer about what was going on. I also couldn't get my door open. It stayed that way for fifty-nine days. John Fund, an editorial writer from *The Wall Street Journal,* heard about the incident and flew all the way to Little Rock to see for himself.

As lieutenant governor, it took me four months to get office letterhead. Every time I sent in a requisition, it was returned because it had the "wrong department number" on it, or the "old number," or an "invalid number," or "too many numbers." I finally had to have the lieutenant governor's letterhead printed at my own expense.

⋆ ⋆ ⋆

Shell-shocked

My first day as governor I had no problems with insubordination; the predicament was exactly the opposite. Administrative support people who had stayed over from the previous administration were shell-shocked and exhausted. Many of them had not submitted their résumés for consideration by the incoming senior staff. I found out later they hadn't bothered doing so because they had been told they all would be fired and that submitting their résumés was a waste of time. We immediately encouraged them to reapply for their jobs if they wanted to and assured them they would be given fair consideration.

Traditionally, the matter of who will stay and who will go is settled well before a new governor begins his term. Senior policy advisers and staff generally follow the departing governor out of office, but mid-level staff and support personnel sometimes stay on. Yet except for one or two brief encounters between May 28 and July 15, Governor Tucker had refused to discuss the transition process. There had been no meetings on personnel and no discussion of records management or the orderly transfer of information regarding state business.

In fact, on my first day as governor, there was no information to transfer. In office after office, we found filing cabinets completely empty. Enough files to fill whole rooms had been shredded or otherwise destroyed. The hard disks on every computer had been erased. We had no records of legislation, no personnel files, no financial records, no accounting ledgers, no correspondence files. Nothing.

Gary Underwood immediately organized a team to rebuild our database. Gary had been on my staff when I was a church pastor and helped our congregation build a community television channel. He supervised the collection of everything we needed to keep the office running without any significant interruption. It wasn't what I had expected to be doing our first day on the job, but the entire office, new hires and veterans alike, pitched in to get the job done.

I also received a gracious letter that day from Jim Guy Tucker:

> I want to publicly apologize to Mike Huckabee and to the people of Arkansas. It was wrong and inconsiderate of me to have changed my resignation schedule as I sought to do yesterday. It was a total surprise to a public who has been wonderfully patient and always trusted my word. It sullied the day Mike and his supporters had spent weeks planning and had deserved to enjoy. It surprised legislators and upset what had been a generally smooth transition. I apologize and hope Governor Huckabee as well as our good citizens will accept my sincere regrets.

Rebuilding the files in the days that followed was a lot easier than rebuilding morale. In talking with experienced members of the governor's office staff, it was clear that the work atmosphere these people had endured was nothing to smile about.

One of my points of agreement with Franklin D. Roosevelt was his belief that profanity is not the language of a democracy. In order to help improve the spirit of the office, I immediately banned smoking and swearing in the governor's office, not because I'm a self-righteous prude but because those things kill morale and sap productivity. Everyone, from the most senior staff member to entry-level clerks, deserves courtesy and respect on the job. Cursing at them and blowing smoke in their faces won't do. I also made it clear that I have no patience with people who make sexually inappropriate remarks. What is innocent fun and joking to one person can be uncomfortable or threatening to another.

Longtime staffers in the governor's office were used to being yelled at. I explained that my guiding principle of management leadership is the Golden Rule: Do unto others as you would have them do unto you. If someone makes a mistake and it really upsets him, there is no purpose in my getting upset, too, because he is probably going to be upset enough for both of us. As long as he has learned from it and can move on, my response is, "Let's correct it, let's not repeat it, but let's not kill anybody over it."

The only time I get really upset is when someone makes a mistake that affects me or others but he doesn't care that it does—he's cavalier about it. But otherwise, you can't let mistakes cripple people. Rather than chew their heads off, show them how they can do a better job next time. It's my policy never, ever to chew someone out in front of others. The only time to pull rank and remind people you're in charge is when someone directly challenges the authority that you and you alone have. That is more than an act of insubordination; it is an act of treason and you have to address it immediately and firmly.

Other than that instance, a person who announces to everyone that he's in charge only proves that he's *not* in charge. A leader who is really in charge never has to mention the fact. His authority is based on respect more than anything else. You can't order people to respect you. Your position may put people in a place where they have to do what you say—but do they comply because they want to or because they have to? If people followed my orders only because they had to, they would do the bare minimum. If they respond because they want to—because I treat them the way I'd like to be treated—they're happier, more thorough, more encouraging to others, and always looking for ways to do the job better. In other words, the Golden Rule is good for business.

I found out there were governors before me who had never met the people who worked for them. One staff member told me that after she had worked for a particular governor for two years, she happened to see him at a mall. The governor introduced himself and she said, "Governor, I've worked for you the past two years." He didn't even know who she was!

Now, I don't know all of the people in state government, but if they work for me, I want to know who they are. I began walking around to various parts of the capitol, meeting workers in their offices, introducing myself, looking at pictures of their children, and getting to know them a little.

★   ★   ★

I'm Not the Boss

The changes we made in the office created incredible improvements in the working environment. Once the office staff knew they would be respected, that every job was important, that honest mistakes would be forgiven, that someone cared who they were and what they did, the fears and confusion melted away. It didn't take weeks; it was more a matter of days or even hours. Before the first week was out, staffers from the previous administration were working alongside people who had been my friends for twenty years, with no distinction, no social pecking order, and no baggage from the past. We were well equipped and well inspired to get on with the people's business.

That phrase "the people's business" suggests perhaps the most important point I made to my staff: I don't like being called "boss." I think of us as a team, and I encourage my coworkers to do the same. Of course, the executive branch of the state government must have a chain of command, and ours does. But part of my job is to reaffirm that every job on the staff is important.

So who is "the boss" in state government? The Arkansas state motto, emblazoned on our official seal, is *Regnat Populus*, which is Latin for "The People Rule." The boss is not me but the citizens we serve. On the wall behind my receptionist's desk hangs a picture frame with the words "Our Boss" at the top. Every few weeks we put in a different photo. One week it may be a Girl Scout Troop from Arkadelphia; the next week it might be a teacher in Mount Ida; the next week, a retired farmer in West

Memphis. These are the people we've pledged to serve. All of us pass this picture frame several times a day. It's an effective reminder of our ultimate place in the chain of command.

The same principle holds true when people come to see me. If they come in with tattered clothes and smell bad and clearly have little power and dignity, the one place where they will be respected is in my office. I have no tolerance for those who look down on others. We work for these people! Some folks may make less money than others; they may live in less adequate houses, or they may have poor job skills—but we are their employees.

A big part of dealing with people is to treat others as you would have them treat you. If you don't want people yelling at you, don't yell at people. If you don't want to be betrayed by people, don't betray others. If you don't like being laughed at, don't laugh at others. I believe in servant leadership. And servant leadership is not cracking the whip.

Servant leadership is the highest form of leadership. It's not the same as doormat leadership. To see your role as servant leader is the ultimate biblical model of leadership. I expect our employees to treat others like they want to be treated, that they understand their job is not to be served but to serve, that they are never to be rude. The people out there who call, write, or visit are not our problem, irritation, or interruption; they are our *job*. Our challenge is not to get those people out of the way so that we can do our work; our work is to help those people. Those people are citizens of the state, and they are our bosses.

Regnat Populus.

IV

I s   G o d   a   D e m o c r a t ?

Before being elected lieutenant governor in July 1993, I had spent twelve years as a Baptist pastor: the first six at Immanuel Baptist Church in Pine Bluff, then another six at Beech Street First Baptist Church in Texarkana. When people hear this, they invariably ask how I could have gone from the pulpit into politics. But I think my life was always headed for politics, although for a time it was diverted to the pastorate.

As a teenager, I was far more interested in politics or broadcasting than in the ministry. Even after I left Southwestern Baptist Theological Seminary in Fort Worth, I didn't see myself headed into a pastorate, but into a ministry in communications or something else outside the traditional pastoral role.

I had been in the advertising business in Fort Worth after college and seminary but had been preaching since I was fifteen.

One Sunday in 1980, I was invited to speak at Immanuel Church in Pine Bluff. The church invited me back to hold a revival, then asked me to serve as its interim pastor, and then to stay on permanently. I spent six good years there before accepting a call from Beech Street First Baptist.

My ministry in Pine Bluff was unconventional because my background was in communications, not traditional ministry. So rather than have a typical visitation program, we advertised on bus benches. I did a radio program each day called "Positive Alternatives" that was designed to be more motivational and inspirational than it was religious. We launched a television channel in Pine Bluff and another station in Texarkana that focused more on local community concerns than on religious ones. We included religious programming, but we also covered high school football and featured talk shows about community events.

It was during this time of ministry that I was gaining maturity and knowledge I would need for a life in public service.

★ ★ ★

Politics in the Church

Whoever said, "politics and religion don't mix" was not a regular churchgoer. I soon discovered that there is an amazing amount of politics in church.

In 1989 I was elected president of the Arkansas Baptist State Convention, the youngest in its 150-year history. With 490,000 members, it is the largest organization of any kind in the state. During my two years as president, the Southern Baptist denomination was undergoing a dramatic change. Traditional, conservative leaders succeeded their more liberal predecessors, and in the process the two sides displayed some of the most intense hardball politics I have ever seen. Some of it was far more brutal than secular politics, in part because in secular politics you *expect* deception and backstabbing; whereas in church politics the common belief is that people are going to behave like Jesus. When they behave more like Beelzebub, you're stunned. In church politics, you're surprised when people are bad, while in secular politics you're surprised when people are good.

In retrospect, I believe Baptist politics paved the way for my later political campaigns. As head of the largest organized group in the state during a tumultuous time, I had the benefit of a lot of media attention. That exposure opened doors for me that wouldn't have opened otherwise, attracting the attention of state Republican Party leaders who expressed an interest in me as a candidate.

I had first gotten interested in the Republicans when I was in high school. I was thirteen in 1968, but I could already tell I was much more in agreement with the conservative Republican viewpoint than I was with Hubert Humphrey's liberalism. By 1972, I was a true-blue, conservative, family-oriented young Republican.

Still, I didn't get involved in party politics while serving as a pastor. I would go to some political dinners or give the invocation at political events, but that was as far as my involvement went. I was certainly open about my personal views, but I never tried to lobby other people in public.

During the time I was president of the Arkansas Baptist State Convention, a couple of my Republican friends asked if I had ever considered running for public office. One of them was Jonathan Barnett. We had met at Boys State (a statewide program for high school boys designed to encourage interest in civic involvement) in 1972, and were both recruited by the state Republican Party to help in the Nixon campaign. I became the southern Arkansas youth coordinator, while he was my counterpart in the northwest. We stayed in contact through the years. I went on to Ouachita Baptist University in Arkadelphia and to seminary in Fort Worth, while he went to John Brown University in Siloam Springs.

Jonathan ran for state representative when he was eighteen. Even though he lost, the campaign whetted his appetite for politics. "Someday you're going to run for governor and I'll help you get elected," he told me a little later.

We first discussed the U.S. Senate race early in 1991. I had been growing restless and frustrated in the ministry, asking more and more what there was of significant, eternal value resulting from all the work the church was doing and all the money it was spending. I could point to some accomplishments, but was the output worth the input?

In my early years of ministry I was quite idealistic, thinking that most people in the congregation expected me to be the captain of a warship leading God's troops into battle to change the world. As the years passed, I became increasingly convinced that most people wanted me to captain the Love Boat, making sure everyone was having a good time. Too many people seemed unconcerned about how many marriages were salvaged, how many kids got off drugs, or how many teen pregnancies were prevented. Rather, the chief concerns seemed to be whether the menus for Wednesday night dinners were appetizing, what color the softball jerseys would be, how loud some guest musicians might sing, whether the coffeepot was ready in the Sunday school building, and whether there were paper towels in the women's rest room.

I grew increasingly frustrated. I wasn't bitter or angry; I just wanted my life to count for something more than as an ordained cruise director. In the U.S. Senate, I thought, a person could make a significant contribution in deciding issues that affect the entire world.

I had to decide whether I would walk away from a comfortable income and career. As a pastor I was set for life. I was pastoring a 2,500-member church at age thirty-five. I had a television ministry (the church had its own studio and transmission tower). I had a generous salary, good benefits, an excellent retirement package—all in all, I probably had more expendable income than I do now as governor. (I certainly didn't go into politics for the money!)

My wife and I had long talks about what to do. Janet and I were married after our freshman year at Ouachita when we were just eighteen. In all the years since, she has been my best friend and confidante. One night, after struggling for weeks about what to do, we took a long walk around our neighborhood, talking and trying to sort things out. If the goal of being a Christian was to be comfortable, we had arrived. But was that where we were supposed to stay? Could I simply say, "I'm a believer" and then kick back and take the world as it came? Jesus told us to be salt and light so our lives might have some kind of impact that will improve the world.

We made our decision that night. The following Sunday, I announced my plans to resign from the ministry, effective the first Sunday in February.

Senator Dale Bumpers would be up for re-election in 1992. He had been governor when I was governor of Boys State in 1972. In fact, he had told me then, "You know, we need young men like you in politics. I hope you will consider that some day." (I quoted his words in speeches when I ran against him.) He had come out of the little town of Charleston, Arkansas, and was considered a fresh face, a young crusader for reform.

Bumpers made a good governor. He had been able to pass legislation stalled for four years by stubborn Democrats because it was proposed by his predecessor, Winthrop Rockefeller, the first Republican elected governor since Reconstruction. Bumpers defeated J. William Fulbright in the 1974 Senate race and went to Washington as a moderate southern Democrat. Bumpers won by convincing the voters that Fulbright was too liberal and that "we need someone with our values." Oddly enough, Bumpers became increasingly liberal once he went to Washington.

Still, whether I could beat an incumbent Democratic senator as a Republican newcomer was a big question, regardless of the man's record. With few exceptions, including the term of Governor Frank White in 1981–82, the Republican Party in Arkansas had been on life support since Reconstruction. In the aftermath of the carpetbaggers, Republicans had been branded as the elite, button-down, wealthy few, and the Democrats as the party of the working man. But in the last few decades the Democrats had become the party of pro-abortionists, gay rights supporters, and others who ignore the bedrock tenets of biblical integrity and long-cherished American traditions. Many Arkansas Democrats weren't comfortable with the new regime.

I also knew that becoming a Republican Party candidate would mean facing unjust opposition and burning some bridges.

☆ ☆ ☆

Anger, Anger Everywhere

When you're a pastor, you make a few people angry, but most of them keep it to themselves. A few bold ones might express their anger at Sunday dinner or in an anonymous letter. But even those who are really angry with you don't write about it in the newspaper or talk about it on TV.

As soon as I announced I was running for the Senate, however, I was fair game. A candidate becomes something less than a person in that anybody can say anything they want to about you. You soon learn that you're a public figure and you can't defend everything, so you just have to live with it.

Another blow was delivered by the church I served. When I announced my intention to run for office, the church quickly decided to call for a vote on extending my health insurance for the rest of the calendar year, a generous offer. I was preaching somewhere else the night the issue came up for a vote, but unfortunately my children were present. To this day they remember vividly what happened. Church members whom we counted as friends—the very people who had asked me to preach at their husband's funeral or whom I had visited in the hospital, those I had comforted through illness, whom I had counseled through crisis—stood up as if I were a total stranger and said, "Well, I don't think we owe him a dime. If he wants to go off and be a Republican, that's his business. It is none of our concern to worry about his health insurance. Nobody is paying for mine."

Many years of friendship and fellowship were damaged in a single night. People we had poured our hearts into in ministry—families coping with the death of a parent or struggling with drug-addicted children—openly campaigned for my opponent solely because he was a Democrat. After you have been through the most intense, intimate crisis with someone, you'd think there would be some kind of bond deeper than affiliation with a certain political party. Yet there wasn't. It was hard for us to accept.

We had to work through a lot of things; that was part of our character building. I try to help my children understand that when people say or write ugly things about you, you're going to have a reaction. But don't let it stay with you because then you will become like they are, and we can't afford that. The experience helped them understand that whenever you take a stance, you pay a price for it.

★　　★　　★

Counting the Cost

At that time my income came from freelance communications work, motivational talks, and speaking in churches. I lost track of the number of times I was scheduled to preach in a Southern Baptist church that year and then got a call from the pastor the week I was supposed to come. He'd say the deacons had met and decided that if I came to speak, they were going to fire the pastor for having a Republican in the pulpit. It was just that plain. It wasn't that I was a *politician*; it was that I was a *Republican*.

Now remember, I had been well accepted as president of our state Baptist convention. I had spoken in most of these churches before and had always been welcome. But suddenly I became tainted merchandise. It was an extremely painful time, especially hurtful to my family. My wife and I both had trouble accepting that people who we thought were our friends never spoke to us again.

Christians often complain about corruption in government and declining morals. You'd think they would have been pleased to have one of their own running for the Senate. But instead of thinking, *We're sending a missionary*, they thought, *we've lost a soul.*

I didn't understand such reasoning. I still don't. People said things like, "Politics is dirty. Christians shouldn't get involved in it." To which I responded, "Everybody wants to eat from a clean plate, but somebody has to do the dishes." It's pointless to gripe about how bad the government is and how terrible the laws are if people who have better ideas are not willing to share them and get involved.

Many Arkansans would have been pleased with what I was doing had I done it as a Democrat. People asked me how many of the Baptists were active in my campaign, and I'd say, "All of them. Half for me and half against." I've never felt such extraordinary hostility and sheer anger. People literally got in my face and yelled.

We were campaigning in Malvern one day and a woman came up to me and said, "I can't vote for you."

"I understand that you *won't*, but you *can't?*" I replied. "You aren't a convicted felon, are you?"

"No, I'm not."

"Are you not registered in Arkansas?"

"No, I'm a registered voter."

"Well, why can't you vote for me?"

"I'm a Democrat, and I'm a Southern Baptist."

I could tell by this woman's attitude that I had nothing to lose, so I said, "Really? I've always wanted to meet someone who is a Southern Baptist like me but who thinks that taking the life of an unborn child was OK."

"Well, I don't believe that."

I said, "Your party does. I also find it curious that we should share the same spiritual roots but that you would believe that men marrying men would be acceptable."

She said, "I don't believe that."

I said, "Your party is advocating that." I mentioned a couple of other issues that were in the Democratic platform in 1992. The news frustrated her, and she finally barked, "Well, I just want you to know that I'm a Democrat," and stalked off. In other words, don't confuse politics with integrity.

I also got hate mail from total strangers. Typically they would start out, "I am a Southern Baptist, but . . . ." and then, boy, saddle up and get ready for a bumpy ride:

> "If you were listening to God, you wouldn't be getting into politics. You've abandoned your call!"
>
> "How can you call yourself a Christian when you don't even realize that you are lowering yourself to a position below your calling?"
>
> "You're *not* called of God. If you were, you wouldn't be a *Republican!*"

★ ★ ★

From Pulpit to Politics

Yet contrary to the opinion of some, I do not believe there is a huge chasm between careers in church and politics. In fact, I would say there is no better preparation for public office than the pastoral ministry. Pastors and politicians have a lot more in common than a closet full of dark suits. They must master the same four skills to succeed:

1. *The ability to communicate a message effectively.* You must be able to articulate your feelings, plans, goals, and mandates clearly to your audience. If you can't communicate, it doesn't matter how worthy your ideas are. They'll die on the vine. Nobody will embrace an idea he can't understand.

2. *The ability to motivate volunteers.* If you can't motivate volunteers, you can't lead a church and you can't run a campaign. Both depend on the enthusiasm and dedication of hundreds or thousands of people who can walk away at any minute. Your only power over them is whatever power they're willing to give you, and they can take it back whenever they want.

3. *A clear understanding of the media.* You must know how the media works, how to use it effectively, how to harness its influence for your benefit. Whether it's a lectern at the Kiwanis Club or the set of a network television show, you have to be relaxed, confident, and secure. Without this, communication is impossible. So many good people fail here because they insist they "shouldn't have to be a star" to make their point. Maybe they shouldn't, but that's

what our society demands of its public figures, whether it's in church or on CNN.

4. *The ability to raise money.* Churches and political campaigns are both built with voluntary contributions. If you can't raise money, you can't lead a church any more than you can win public office.

Beyond these four key skills, other elements are much the same for both pastors and politicians.

First, you'll never please everybody in either role. You have to deal with issues and make decisions based on information you can't share with anyone because to do so would violate a confidence. And often, while the decision and implementation might be simple, the thinking behind that decision is anything but simple. You have to make decisions knowing they will be misunderstood, questioned, and often maligned by people who don't know all the facts.

Second, as an officeholder, you're responsible for spending public funds wisely when taxpayers will probably never know if you're wasting their money. As a pastor, I knew there were widows in our church who were tithing on their Social Security checks. Whenever I spent money from the church budget, I needed to think I could look those women in the eyes and say, "I think we spent that money wisely. We have taken good care of what you have entrusted to us." It's the same thing in politics. A public official does not spend his own money. In the church we raise funds through voluntary contributions, while the government gets its money through taxation. Yet in neither case is the money mine. Can I look the citizens of Arkansas in the eyes and say, "We've been responsible with what we took from you. We needed that money and spent it wisely in your best interest"? Good stewardship is very much a part of both politics and the pastorate.

Third, both pastors and politicians must have the ability to persuade people to adopt their point of view. Pastoral and political power are both based on volunteers and voluntary contributions. You can't hold a hammer over your people's heads. Church councils and legislative councils both have to inspire their constituents to follow the direction they set.

Last, families of ministers and those of elected officials are held to different standards than everybody else. I've lived most of my adult life in a fishbowl. Right or wrong, Janet, John Mark, David, and Sarah are put under a public microscope and scrutinized every day. There is a sense in which we're never "off." People expect us to play a certain role once we leave our private quarters. We have to be comfortable with being who we are and must beware of building up some kind of false "public" personality. I think there is a difference between role-playing and role-living. Role-playing is a sham; role-living is being comfortable with who you are anytime an observer walks up to the fishbowl for a look.

And they *will* look—especially when the fishbowl features a few Republicans swimming in a largely Democratic state, but even more so when those Republican "fish" claim ultimate allegiance not to a party, but to the living God.

Let me be clear. The Republican Party is not "God's party" either. God doesn't join our organizations; He asks us to join His. Political parties are simply vehicles to help us get to the place of changing public policy, and some vehicles drive better than others because of their features.

V

★ ★ ★

Y e l l o w   D o g s   B i t e

Republican candidates have a tough time campaigning in Arkansas. During the 1992 race, I often had the worst seat at banquets and fish fries and was pointedly ignored by event organizers. In parades, my car was put at the end of the line behind the horses, along with the street sweeper and the fire truck. They would literally hold my car back as the other candidates pulled into position, then send me in last. They didn't even try to be subtle about it.

The Clinton presidential race dominated media coverage that year. His national campaign headquarters was in Little Rock, which meant reporters from around the world were camped out there to cover the campaign. It was the first time an Arkansan had ever been a major party nominee for president, and voter turnout in the state was off the charts. The downside was that every day, news about the Senate race was at the bottom of the front page or halfway through a TV newscast. We just couldn't make enough noise.

The bad news was that we lost the race. The good news was that we got 40 percent of the vote even though we were heavily outspent and even though an Arkansas Democrat was elected president. George Bush's approval rating just after Desert Storm had been 91 percent, and he lost the White House. Compared with that, 40 percent didn't look so terrible.

Even in defeat, we got credit for running a credible race that left the door open for future opportunities. It showed that I had an army of true-blue supporters. Dick Morris, who became my pollster, said he had never polled anyone whose supporters were so fanatically loyal. "Your voters would swim the Mississippi at flood stage to get to the ballot box on election day," he told me. They would never believe something bad in the news or opinion pages about me because they knew what I stood for and they stood for the same things.

When Bill Clinton was elected president, his lieutenant governor, Jim Guy Tucker, became governor under the terms of the state constitution. Then there had to be a special election for lieutenant governor. Since we already had a dedicated, loyal staff that had proved itself in the Senate race, we decided I should enter the field. The combination of my service at the Baptist Convention and the Senate campaign had given me a higher profile than any Republican had enjoyed in years. Still, it was an uphill battle.

There is a particular kind of voter in the South called a yellow dog Democrat—a person who will vote Democratic even if the candidate is a yellow dog. Though many people agreed with my positions on the issues, my party label was more than they could stand. There were newspapers in the state that not only wouldn't cover me as a candidate but would forbid the editor to come out and shake my hand. I'd ride in local parades and well-dressed, middle-aged women would make obscene gestures and yell, "We don't like you and we don't want you here! We're not voting for you!"

Several factors contributed to my victory in the lieutenant governor's race in July 1993. First, our team had just been through the Senate race and had learned so much from the experience. Second, we had a clear, consistent message of honesty and integrity that resonated with voters. Third, we took our opponents by surprise. They had campaigned against weak opposition for so long that they weren't prepared to take us on.

Yet even as lieutenant governor, I had those yellow dogs on my tail all the time. Wayne Hogan, a friend in the office supply business, loaned me a desk for the lieutenant governor's office because, once I got the door un-nailed, there was no furniture inside and I couldn't get any. I often got on an elevator at the capitol and people got out; they refused to ride with me.

During my first year in office, I went to a big summer festival in south Arkansas that politicians always attend. When I got there, they told me to "just sit anyplace you can find." The only place left was in the back of the room. All other elected officials were up on stage to be introduced, including the state senator who was planning to challenge me when I ran for re-election in 1994. So they introduced the various guests, including this state senator, whom they called "our next lieutenant governor." After they had introduced everybody (down to the quorum court members) they said, "We do have some other members here in our audience, including a Republican, Mike Huckabee." *A Republican.* They didn't even mention that I was the sitting lieutenant governor.

These sorts of incidents actually helped me get reelected in 1994. The Democrats unintentionally transformed me from a vile Republican to a friend of the common folk. People in Arkansas really do have a genuine sense of fairness and propriety. They may be yellow dog Democrats, but deep down there were a lot of people who seemed to say, "I didn't vote for him, I don't like Republicans, but he won the election—so let's treat him right." They were embarrassed for their own party at the kind of treatment I was receiving, and the sympathy worked in our favor.

★ ★ ★

The Tucker-Clinton Rivalry

Jim Guy Tucker and I were nothing alike, but initially I had a very good working relationship with him. In fact, I had a much better working relationship with Tucker than he had experienced with Governor Clinton. The two of them had been rivals for years. I know a person doesn't understand Arkansas politics when I hear him talking about how Tucker and Clinton were tied together in a Whitewater conspiracy. Bill Clinton and Jim Guy Tucker mistrusted each other far too much to be partners in any sort of business deal. Privately, neither would say a nice thing about the other. They barely spoke, much less worked together.

Their rivalry went back to 1978 when Clinton was the attorney general running for governor and Tucker was a congressman running for the Senate. They toyed with the idea of running against each other for either senator or governor and kind of danced around the ring, shadow boxing. Clinton ran for governor and won; Tucker ran for the Senate and lost. In 1982, when Clinton was making his comeback after having been voted out of office in 1980, Tucker ran against him in the Democratic primary. Clinton beat Tucker and the bitterness between them intensified.

Tucker returned to the private sector and nearly disappeared until announcing he would run for governor again in 1990. He made that decision because Clinton hinted he wasn't going to run for re-election. Taking the cue, Tucker announced his candidacy and spent $100,000 getting the ball rolling.

Then Clinton called a press conference in the rotunda of the state capitol. Dick Morris told me later that the purpose of the event was for Clinton to announce he wasn't going to run for reelection. That was the news everybody was expecting and it was what Clinton planned to say. But as he spoke to his supporters, he could not bring himself to declare he wasn't running. Not even Hillary realized what was going to happen. In the middle of his speech, he went from setting up the announcement that he wasn't going to run to saying, "I'm going to run, one more time."

Tucker was devastated. He knew he couldn't beat Clinton, so he backed out of the governor's race to run for lieutenant governor, a position in Arkansas that is about as attractive to career politicians as the spit collector in a boxing ring. The lieutenant governor presides over some meetings and has some ceremonial functions, but as far as Tucker was concerned, it was just a perfunctory position. It was a real step down for him.

I've heard people say they suspect Clinton and Tucker made some sort of deal: "Back off and let me get reelected, then you can move up when I become president." They would never have trusted each other enough for that.

When Clinton became president, Tucker was thrust into the governor's office; but even before that, during the 1992 presidential campaign, Tucker was the *de facto* governor because Clinton was never there. Clinton was not terribly interested in staying governor after 1990. He was running for president the whole time.

What really bothered Tucker was that Clinton would hand unfinished business to him but never give him the inside information he needed to handle it well. It was a tough time. Increasingly as Clinton got into the presidential campaign, Tucker had more day-to-day impact on managing the government.

When Clinton moved to the White House after the 1992 election, Tucker was furious with him. Clinton left the state in a financial mess, which Tucker had to clean up. Tucker took office on Saturday, December 12, 1992, and called a special session on Monday, December 14, to deal with a state Medicaid funding shortage.

★ ★ ★

Tucker's Tactics

During Tucker's first months as governor, he and I had a good working relationship. I went out of my way to support things I thought were good. I tried not to be too partisan, and I think he genuinely appreciated my efforts. It was lonely being a Republican in the capitol, but we got along all right.

Things went sour in 1995 amidst increasing talk that Tucker was going to be indicted by the Whitewater grand jury. The special prosecutor was really squeezing him. When the indictment came down in June of 1995, I was careful not to say anything negative. In fact, I was supportive of him; he was innocent until proven guilty. And he was still the state's chief executive.

With all the controversy and talk of felony charges, Governor Tucker knew early in the year he needed to do something to give him the appearance of a strong, visionary, well-respected leader. To do that he pushed three major issues in 1995. Unfortunately, they were three poorly conceived pieces of legislation. The year became a bloodbath that resulted in exactly the opposite impression Tucker was hoping for.

His three big programs were (1) a total change of the public school funding system; (2) a highway construction program; and (3) a rewrite of the state constitution. All three were unpopular with the public.

Tucker's ill-received education plan involved consolidating the state's 311 school districts into thirty-five super districts. When he tried to address a big crowd in Cabot on the issue, they almost booed him off the rostrum. I support local school districts, thinking, *If people are happy with it, who are we to try and tell them they can't have their own school?* The governor's thought was, *These country schools need to be brought into districts with the big city ones, even though country schools are more efficient.*

His highway bill was the worst mess I'd ever seen. It called for the biggest tax increase in state history and huge bonded indebtedness, but he insisted that the legislature vote to hold a public referendum on it. He finally squeezed enough votes to hold the referendum, where he played Santa to the senators, bringing them in one at a time and asking, "And what do you want in your district?"

"Well, I got to have a new gym for my college."

"I have to have your vote on the highway bill."

"OK."

These senators would go back to their seats and call out, "I'll vote for it." And when they got the eighteenth person in the thirty-five-member Senate to agree, they called for the vote and passed it. I could hardly believe the number of people who told me to my face that this was the worst piece of legislation they had ever seen but voted for it anyway. Holding a public referendum cost the state a million dollars.

The governor's plan for a constitutional convention was originally an inclusive process. He had asked me, along with other Republicans, to work with him so we could examine all sides of the issues freely and openly. Then one night I'd been invited to speak at a Methodist church in Jonesboro. Tucker reached me by cellular phone and essentially told me that everything I had been promised was off. There was no way the Democrats were going to let me have any significant role in the constitutional convention, although that statement violated everything we had agreed upon.

What had happened? The governor had caved in to political pressure.

By this time, I had announced that I was going to run for Senate in 1996. The Democrats didn't want to do anything to make me look good, whether it was advising the governor on education reform or being part of a constitutional convention. "This is not what we agreed," I told the governor. "I think you're going to need broad support to make changes in the constitution."

"I don't need your support," he replied. It would be his way or no way. There was no negotiation, no discussion.

I said, "Do what you want, but I can't support you. I have no confidence in this."

In 1996, Arkansas would have an open seat in the U.S. Senate for the first time in eighteen years, and I was ready to go for it. Even though the Whitewater investigation was underway, I didn't think Tucker was guilty and never thought he would be indicted. If he were to go to trial and be convicted, I assumed appeals would drag on for years. By the time it would positively affect the lieutenant governor's position, I thought, I would be long gone to Washington.

In December 1995, the referendum on the constitutional convention failed 80 percent to 20 percent, one of the worst, most lopsided defeats in state history. Tucker put his credibility on the line and got hammered. That made him angry. He blamed me in part for the failure because I had opposed him.

The highway vote was next, scheduled for the following month. I opposed it because of its cost and because it contained so many critical flaws. Not only that, but the Republican Party spent about $200,000 for me to oppose it on TV. Of course, Tucker went ballistic. He was trying to promote this highway program while a TV spot for the opposition featured me as its spokesman. Yet I never attacked him personally; I opposed the highway program exclusively.

The highway referendum lost 87 percent to 13 percent, an even worse defeat than the constitutional convention. The political cartoonists had a field day portraying Tucker as a "lame duck." He wanted to go into his trial looking like a strong, visionary leader who had the support of the people of Arkansas. Instead, he went into that trial having been whipped worse than almost any governor in history in two special elections.

At any time Tucker could have compromised, if only he had realized how out of touch he was and how strongly the people opposed his plans. I think he also got bad advice; his chief adviser was a close friend who was as out of touch with reality as Tucker. Even worse, Tucker had developed a dangerously inflated opinion of his political judgment. He had gotten so focused on the idea of going into his trial with a shining legacy that he developed tunnel vision. He'd lose, but he wouldn't quit. He was absolutely immovable. He would not compromise.

Then when his legislative efforts were defeated, rather than accept responsibility for what happened, he blamed me—particularly for the highway bill. After the defeat of the highway referendum, I saw him only twice for photo op meetings during the rest of my tenure as lieutenant governor. Aside from those two brief meetings, the next time I heard his voice was on July 15, telling me he had decided not to resign.

Leaders have the responsibility to think and act in the context of their positions. Having been awarded their offices by voters, elected officials in particular must consider the effect their actions will have on others. In trying to pursue his interests rather than the interests of his constituents, Governor Tucker found his own people turned against him. Even yellow dog Democrats had had enough.

VI

* * *

U n d e r   t h e   I n f l u e n c e

Each of us is the product of many influences, some major, some less important. It's like making stew. There may be more potatoes than tomatoes, but every ingredient makes a difference. When it is all finished, a unique flavor results.

Many people have been key ingredients in my life. The first ones were my parents, working-class people who struggled to make ends meet but who were grateful for what they had and made the most of it. They represented about as pure an America as there is. They had a better life than their parents, but they wanted a better life for their children. They worked hard and carefully instilled a solid work ethic in my sister and me, insisting that no one was going to hand us anything. If we wanted something, we knew we were going to have to work for it.

⋆ ⋆ ⋆

Teaching by Example

Then there were my teachers. I was fortunate to have an out-standing public education. My teachers in Hope were good people and dedicated instructors. They instilled in me a desire to learn. They introduced us to the biographies of great people, books that had a major influence on me. I read every biography I could find from the second grade on. (Sad to say, many of the biographies written today dwell on the scandalous and irrepons-sible episodes in a person's life rather than on the accomplish-ments that earned a person fame. There was no way we ever would have been exposed to the sexual indiscretions of Dwight Eisenhower. He was a great general and a fine president, a posi-tive influence on our culture.)

In high school, teachers had even more of an impact on me. One I particularly remember is Alex Strawn, the speech, drama, and debate coach. He was a young teacher—it was his first assignment—and bursting with idealism, eager to inspire young minds. We were impressionable kids just waiting for someone like him to come along. It was a wonderful combination. He developed a debate program that challenged every brain cell. He pushed us in just the right way to be our best.

Another memorable teacher was Anna E. Williams, the stu-dent council adviser. She took me under her wing. From the ninth grade, when I was a student council representative, to twelfth grade, when I was council president, she kept pushing me to do better and to get more done. Mrs. Williams was determined to develop leadership skills in me. She made me visit her every morning before school for half an hour. I'd have to go through my goals for that day and give account for my goals from the day before. She was a list maker and turned me into one.

Today I am a fanatic list maker. And it works. I can tell how good a day I've had by how many things I can check off. This practice of making lists instilled in me a sense of establishing priorities and tracking progress. Mrs. Williams pushed me. No matter how much I accomplished, she would always point out what more I could have done with a little more effort. I look back now and realize she was instilling in me disciplines useful throughout life.

Attending Ouachita Baptist University was an outstanding experience for me. It allowed me to take on the challenge of being with some of the sharpest high school graduates in the state. And the peer pressure was wonderful. What a difference between typical secular college peer pressure and the pressure at Ouachita! While the pressure at a secular school might be to skip class or guzzle a six-pack with the guys, the pressure at Ouachita is to excel.

So many students competed for academic awards that the party animals usually didn't last more than a semester or two. Those who stayed were serious when it came to their education. Some of them may have been pranksters, but they didn't go there just to waste four years of their lives. The positive influence of my fellow students was, in part, what helped me get through a four-year program in a little more than two years.

At fourteen I held my first job, working at the radio station in Hope. Haskell Jones, the station manager, was a powerful influence in my life. First, he gave me an opportunity to work.

Second, he was very patriotic. If "The Star-Spangled Banner" played on the radio, he would stand up and put his hand over his heart. He instilled in everybody who knew him the idea that the American dream was something to be cherished. He was also one of the few Republicans I knew in Hope. He was true to his beliefs; he didn't care that everyone thought he was a little loony for being a Republican. He was one, and that was the way it was.

Mr. Jones was probably the most community-minded person I have ever known. Whenever there was a need, we would do radiothons. If there was some little girl who was desperately ill and needed a transplant or special treatment, Mr. Jones would see to it. This was before health insurance became so prevalent, and these were proud southern people. If somebody was in need, we'd spend a whole Saturday on the radio raising money. I just assumed everybody thought you should give something back to your community—through the chamber of commerce, United Way, or a civic club. I've tried to follow his example; I've always been involved in community organizations and projects.

As I look back, it's hard to imagine someone who would turn a radio station over to a fourteen-year-old kid. I would be there all by myself. I'd turn the transmitter on in the morning, do the news and the weather, and play records. At our church's television station in Texarkana, I wouldn't let a fourteen-year-old answer the phone, much less run the whole station!

* * *

Growing Up in Church

I grew up in a small Missionary Baptist church, and at the time the theology that dominated those churches in the South was somewhat legalistic. Although today I believe this emphasis is misguided, it probably protected me from dangerous experiments that damaged peers.

The other side of the coin was that there was a heavy emphasis on Scripture, Bible study, and memorization, all of which will serve me for the rest of my life. My pastors and Sunday school teachers had a big influence on me. Some were particularly helpful in getting me to see the value of Scripture. I was inquisitive and liked to ask questions about "why can't we?" or "why is it wrong?" I was not satisfied when the answers were, "You're just not supposed to."

"Well, why? Why is that wrong?"

"Because . . . it's just not the way we are supposed to do it."

When I was fourteen or fifteen, I went through a period of disenchantment with such non-answers. I know it's tempting to say, "Because the Bible says it's wrong," and leave it at that. But there are reasons *why* the Bible says it's wrong, and there are rational, appropriate foundations for the prohibitions we find in God's Word. Part of my rebellion was toward this can't-do mentality. I wanted to know what I *could* do. Tell me something that is positive, tell me something that is worthy of my life, something I can invest myself in. Don't just give me a list of restrictions!

My own experience has taught me that we can't get by with telling teenagers, "Just because!" when it comes to spiritual matters. We need to give them the principles behind the rules. They may not agree with them, but at least we have given them a basis to understand the "why" when we tell them not to drink or whatever.

My early struggle with legalism greatly affected my walk with the Lord. Today I am definitely a "grace Christian" and not a "law Christian." One of the few things I detest more than liberalism is legalism. I think both are cancers to the Christian faith—liberalism because it doesn't believe anything, and legalism because it restricts us only to the things we can live up to. Liberalism makes God seem so commonplace that He becomes meaningless, while legalism makes God so small that He becomes insignificant.

The negative aspect of a legalistic worldview is that you create what becomes your own Christian faith. It's really a set of do's and don'ts that allow someone to judge whether others are good people or good Christians. The problem is, we're always going to create a list we can live up to—which means we're not living up to the standards of Jesus Christ. We are merely living up to the standards of our list, which is a form of self-idolatry. "Don't smoke, don't drink, pet your dog every day—if you can do all those things, then you redeem yourself" even though your life may be filled with jealousy, greed, lust, and every other deadly vice.

Dealing with situations as a pastor, I became keenly aware of our utter failure as human beings to live up to the pure standard of God. Even the best people I knew fell hopelessly short, which convinced me even more of the need for grace. I came to understand the importance of the cross, the divine bridge between God and man. I grew up with *The Four Spiritual Laws* and knew about the big gap between us and God—but hearing that and seeing it in people's lives are two different things. Fortunately, God is gracious. And just as He exercises grace toward me, I have to exercise grace toward others. It's easy to want Him to exercise grace toward me; the real reach is becoming anxious for Him to exercise grace toward others.

Today, grace affects everything I think and do. In every decision I make as a governor, as a father, a spouse, a friend, it has an impact on me. When I think of Anna Williams, Haskell Jones, and other important people in my life, I remember both their inspiring encouragement and their eagerness to see me succeed. God gave them to me as examples of how we can grant grace to each other. I pray I never lose sight of the lesson they taught.

VII

J a n e t

I have heard that people often marry their opposites. It's certainly true in my marriage. I like to engage in thoughtful discourse on why we are doing something, trying to clarify our goals; Janet just wants to get it done. I will take nonphysical risks, such as running for office or taking a job that may not work out; Janet will take physical risks—climbing cliffs, parasailing, racing cars, or stalking bears.

Janet's sense of adventure attracted me when we were both high school students in Hope. Another attraction was her spiritual strength. People can provide some of the moral anchors we need in life, and my most extraordinary anchor is Janet.

My wife's physical stamina and moral strength were shaped by challenges she faced early in life. Her father left her family (Janet, her mother, two brothers, and two sisters) when she was a child. Her mother had no choice but to tough it out. They had to stretch a single, modest paycheck to cover all six of them.

Janet grew up learning to be frugal, what it means to share, and developing a lot of independence. In her life, the mother was the primary role model, so she had quite a different perspective of family responsibilities than I had. Even today, if something needs to be fixed, she fixes it.

I am utterly inept when it comes to mechanical things. My father, on the other hand, was a talented mechanic. He liked physical labor. He did everything from wiring houses to putting out fires, and on his days off he was a mechanic in his little generator shop. If something needed to be done around the house, he would do it. He could fix things much better than he could explain to a child how to do it. Rather than, "Let me show you how," he'd say, "Just let me get this done." Consequently, I appreciate the fact that Janet can change tires.

Another episode in her life also helps to account for her courage and strength. During the first year of our marriage, she was diagnosed with cancer of the spine. That was a traumatic time in our lives, but her resolve carried her through. Despite the doctors' dire predictions, she completely recovered.

Janet's faith and stamina were tested again three years after John Mark was born. She became pregnant again but miscarried after about three months. Rather than letting the tragedy of that loss consume her, she came out of it even stronger. Her faith was unshaken.

She ended up learning and growing through all of it. Otherwise, I'm not sure how she would have reacted to a husband who went from communications to the pastorate to politics.

* * *

Tender Heart but Tough As Nails

Janet is also fearless and has a tough exterior to protect the inside, which is, frankly, vulnerable. Don't get me wrong. She's not tough in the sense of cruel—people love her when they get to know her—but she's tough in that she will stand up for herself and others when she feels someone is being abused or marginalized. She has a sensitive heart for people who are being abused and abhors it when someone looks down his nose at someone else.

For her, one of the most difficult aspects of being Arkansas' first lady was the inevitable confrontation with some of the snobby elitists who had always been on the side of the culturally correct in Little Rock. We're a little more informal, and we make no excuses for it. Janet also has to contend with nitpickers about everything from what she wears to what furniture she moves in the governor's mansion. It just goes with the territory, and she handles it with admirable grace.

One of Little Rock's liberal, cynical newspaper columnists wrote a piece about Janet's doings at the mansion, so she called him up and asked, "Have you been to the mansion lately? Why don't you just come over here, and I'll show you what's going on." She spent an hour and a half taking him all over the place, even up in the attic. That's her style. She didn't sit around and brood about it. She called invited him to see what the real situation was.

If being a wife in the public fishbowl is tough, being a mother is worse. It presents all kinds of challenges for her. I think the best preparation my children could have had for playing the role of "the governor's kids" was being "the preacher's kids." John Mark is almost twenty-one now, David is seventeen, and Sarah is fifteen; their whole lives people have expected them to be either perfect or horrible. If they act up, I hear, "Hey, what do you expect? They're the preacher's kids." Or folks expect them to be perfect and are flabbergasted when they aren't: "I can't believe you would do that when your *father* is a *pastor*." It's exactly the same when your father is governor. And, of course, Janet feels the full force of these harsh comments when they hit.

Our kids are also used to having their father criticized and critiqued by people who don't know the facts. Before, it was a barbed comment about a sermon. Now, it's about a speech or policy decision. The situation is intensified, the light is hotter, the audience is bigger, but it's basically the same. The major difference is that in church, although they put you on a pedestal and scrutinize you as you swim around the fishbowl, they really want you to succeed because you are their model. In politics, they also put you on a pedestal, but there they want you to fall. They want to take comfort in knowing you aren't any better than they are.

To overcome some of this oversized scrutiny, Janet and I both do what we can to help our children lead normal lives. For example, our daughter was on a mock trial team in junior high. In the spring of 1997, the team went to the national finals, the first time a junior high team had ever gone from Arkansas. Janet accompanied the team, not as the first lady but as a mother going on a field trip. David likes drama, so we try to see his plays. Because we're parents, Janet and I do a lot of speaking at schools.

★ ★ ★

Raising the Bar

Janet is also an extremely effective fund-raiser. Don't ask her to help unless you are serious; otherwise, she'll wear you out. When the Florence Crittenton Home, a home for unwed mothers in Little Rock, asked for her help, she led an effort that eventually surpassed the previous fund-raising record by $30,000. She headed fund-raising for the Red Cross after the 1997 tornadoes; they set a goal of $100,000 and raised $165,000. She rode in an American Lung Association bike race, biking sixty-three miles in one day from Little Rock to Hot Springs. She currently leads the Shots for Tots campaign in Arkansas. The goal is to get the children of the state immunized. The state health director asked her to head the campaign. Their goal was 90 percent until Janet said, "We'd better make it 95 percent." They changed the goal.

Beyond all doubt, Janet is a person of action. Talking policy bores her; she's interested in implementation. Her philosophy on how to accomplish welfare reform sounds like something from John Wayne: "Saddle up, Pilgrim, and get to work." She is more the type to get down on the floor and play with the kids than to lecture them on the fine art of government. She likes to be involved in the action far more than debate the philosophy behind it.

Once, when Janet was chaperoning a group of graduating high school students a couple of years ago, they went to a place that offered bungee jumping. Some of the students saw it and were thinking about giving it a try, but then they backed down. So Janet said, "Well, I'll do it."

And she did. Twice. I've seen the video.

Part II

* * *

THE NEED
FOR CHARACTER

* * *

VIII

★ ★ ★

The   Moral   Thermostat

In one of our few brief meetings before I assumed the office of governor, Jim Guy Tucker told me about a cabinet member he was going to fire. The governor said he would do me a favor and fire him before I had to take him. I listened and said, "If that is what you think of his work, it's OK with me. He's a nice guy, but I never have evaluated him. It's your call."

Later I was told Tucker's chief of staff called the man in and said, "We've got to fire you because the lieutenant governor wants us to get rid of you before he takes office."

The man immediately came to me and asked, "Did you order me fired?"

I told him I hadn't. He played a tape of the conversation; I was incredulous. "That is absolutely untrue!" I said. "He told me *he* wanted to fire you." I hired the man to head another department, and he has done a splendid job in that position.

I had informed Tucker that I wanted to keep some clerical workers. We wanted at least some people who knew where the bathrooms were. Besides that, we wanted to see how many would like to stay; we didn't want to throw everybody out. Tucker's aides told them, "You are going to lose your jobs. You won't have a job after we leave, so just get ready to go."

We thought employees were being told they could apply to keep their jobs. When we received only three or four résumés out of almost fifty staffers, we knew something wasn't right. Finally a staff member said, "Tucker's chief of staff told us it didn't make any difference what we did, we wouldn't be hired anyway." I was stunned. I asked to meet with the employees and told them that while we couldn't keep policy-level senior staff, we would like some others to stay. They are now some of the most fulfilled, dedicated, outstanding public servants in the state.

✶ ✶ ✶

The Root of Character

Treating people with integrity and respect is the only way to get them to achieve their full potential. And it isn't just a matter of saying character counts and leaving it at that. Character *does* count. Integrity *does* count. But if integrity and character are divorced from God, they don't make sense. If you try to set your own moral thermostat, chances are that a lot of other people will be uncomfortable. Integrity left to define itself becomes evil because everyone ends up choosing his own standards.

One afternoon when my son John Mark was twelve, he didn't want to go shopping with the rest of the family so he stayed home. When we returned, he walked up to me, beaming, and said, "Dad, I did something while you were gone. I made a cake!" This was totally out of character for him. He was so excited, and I was so proud that he had done something unselfish for us. Thinking back to seminars that said "encourage your children, give them lots of praise," I got ready to praise this cake.

He said, "Here. I want you to have the first piece."

It looked pretty good and as I sank my teeth into the first bite, I determined that praise would flow out of my mouth for this wonderfully selfless gift. Unfortunately, only cake flowed out of my mouth as I involuntarily spit it out. That cake was atrocious! *This kid is trying to kill me!* I thought. I asked him, gently, "Did you follow a recipe for this cake?"

"Yes sir," he answered.

"Could I see that recipe?"

"Yes sir."

The recipe looked perfectly acceptable. "Are you sure you followed this recipe exactly?"

"Yes sir, I promise I followed the recipe exactly . . . except for one thing. It said to add a dash of salt. I didn't know what a dash was, but I figured a cup ought to take care of it."

He had put a full cup of salt in his cake. A cow could have licked on it for six months and still had some left.

The point of the story is this: my son's motives were honorable and sincere. His efforts were diligent, and he finished the task he had set out to do following the instructions as he understood them. There was only one problem: no one had defined for him what a "dash" is. It was an unknown standard. He made up his own standard, and the results were utterly disastrous.

In the same way, we're afraid in this country today to define for our children what is right and wrong. Instead, we say, "You'll have to find out for yourself," or "Do whatever seems good for you." We tell them, "It doesn't matter what you believe as long as you are sincere," and "Do your best." Such misguided sentiments are the tragic products of our morally relativistic generation. We believe fairness is more important than accuracy, that effort counts for more than excellence, that participation is as good as achievement.

We are scared to death to say, "That's wrong." We want to say, "You have a disorder or a disability," or any of the scores of euphemisms people use. Yet all we're doing is struggling to cover up immoral, improper, illegal, or boorish behavior.

We try to excuse it. "He was just expressing himself. Don't squash his creativity!" But children need to be disciplined and to know there are lines they must live within.

When a pilot flies into a city, he encounters miles of concrete in all directions; but it is crucial that the pilot land only on a particular strip of concrete to which the air traffic controller directs him. If he lands on the freeway in rush-hour traffic, hundreds of people could die. Is it narrow-minded to limit him to that one strip of concrete? Perhaps so, but anything else leads to disaster.

Our children must be told which concrete is safe to land on. Too often we fail to say, "*This* is right; anything else is wrong." Instead we say, "Wherever you want to go is fine." There are a lot of places in Little Rock where there's room to land a jetliner, and most of them are wrong.

We refuse to direct our children and then run around moaning, "What is wrong with our kids today? Look at the violence!

Look at the decadence! Look at the drug addiction and alcohol addiction and the lack of respect!" Why are we moaning? *We trained them to be this way.*

There has to be an immovable standard. A solid foundation. A moral thermostat whose setting is not subject to the whim of personal opinion.

On March 1, 1997, a tornado cut a 260-mile path of destruction through Arkansas. We went up to Jacksonport, one of the most devastated communities, to survey the damage. As soon as we got off the helicopter, state representative Martha Shoffner of Newport met me and said, "Governor, I've got to show you something you won't believe." We drove into town and entered a museum in the old courthouse. The tornado had torn off most of the roof, and the interior was trashed by the storm.

Everything in the room was either blown away or ruined, except for one item: a picture of me as governor, hanging on the wall. It was still there; it hadn't moved, or even as much as tilted. The thought occurred to me that during all the storms and ferocious pressures that blow into our lives, we must stand firm. You can't stop storms, and you can't hide from them. All you can hope for is that when the storms hit, you are able to stay put.

★   ★   ★

Live Narrowly, Love Broadly

Being a Christian makes it possible to stay put. But I think many well-meaning Christians mistakenly think that because they recognize the value of integrity, they should avoid people who don't. This is a grave error. Christians who understand their faith are not exclusive, but inclusive.

Jesus was the most inclusive person in the world. He lived life within narrowly defined boundaries, but He loved broadly, reaching out to people from every conceivable walk of life. I'm afraid we too often twist that around; we have a broad life and love narrowly. Many contemporary believers love people only like themselves: white, middle-class church members who practice the same habits and avoid the same behaviors. They don't know many people who are Jewish or black, poor or wealthy. What a tragedy.

Being governor gives me an opportunity to practice my faith with a broad range of people. After the tornado, there were practical things I could do to help people rebuild their communities. But I also had the opportunity to bring some sense of consolation, some sense of perspective to the situation. What a privilege to offer hope in the midst of what looked like an utterly hopeless situation.

It's humbling to kneel down and take the hand of an elderly lady sitting in a borrowed lawn chair, in front of what used to be her house. Her husband of forty-two years had been killed in the storm. In many ways I was more of a pastor than a governor during that time. There are times when I feel I'm pastoring a 2.5-million-member church.

Crises like that provide a true test of character. Is there looting, or do neighbors pitch in and help each other? Do victims file accurate claims? Do insurance companies pay promptly? I agree with the writer who said that "character is the person you are when no one is looking." It's the person you are when the cameras are off, the witnesses are gone, and there's no one to keep score.

I think we all are performers to some extent. But the real person is the one who is as nearly the same behind closed doors as in the public eye. We might say, "I'd never steal with someone watching me." But would we steal if no one was watching? We'd never lie if we thought someone might find out; but would we lie if we thought no one would ever know? Those are the real issues of life—not "What can I get by with?" but "What do I want to get by with?"

It seems to me that the desire to see public officials fail the integrity test is at an all-time high. The media is saturated with it. The reason for this, I believe, is that by showing the character flaws in other people, the public affirms that its own inadequacies are really not so abnormal. As the character of America begins to plummet, we want to justify our own lack of morality by somehow showing that everyone is just as bad.

People who lie think everyone is a liar. Thieves think everyone steals. People who are insincere in their comments and actions think everyone else is insincere. Therefore, people who are essentially unethical think everyone is unethical, and they're determined to find it in you. If you're not overtly flawed, you become a contrast and a threat. It's proof of the biblical statement that men are lovers of darkness rather than light, because the light exposes their dark deeds.

I am reminded of when I was a little kid at a church camp in Gary, Texas. There was a 10 P.M. lights-out policy. As soon as the lights were off and the counselor was snoring, the guys would get up, fish out their hidden Cheerios and M&Ms, and start crawling around in the rafters of the barracks. When the counselor heard something and flipped on the lights, everybody would scramble around like cockroaches and jump into the nearest bed. In the dark, we misbehaved; in the light, we hid in fear.

That's what has happened to the public at large. People are desperate to justify their own immoral attitudes by saying, "He's a failure, too, so I'm as good as he is." Our generation has learned to hold to the standard of each other instead of the standard of God. That is the travesty: God is no longer the standard; we are.

IX

The Ultimate Question

There's a continuing debate about why American society has renounced its traditional standards of integrity. Many people agree that as a nation we once recognized a common standard and that somehow we've drifted away from it. The "right thing" today is subjective, which has caused problems with everything from discipline in the schools to pornography on the Internet.

How did we move in one generation from a society with a shared, confident sense of right to a society of relativism and moral decay?

* * *

No Single Answer

The first step to answering that question is to admit there isn't just one answer. I've heard that it all started when we took prayer out of schools. That's a simplistic answer. It wasn't just prayer in schools; it wasn't just television; it wasn't just Watergate; it wasn't just welfare. It wasn't any one thing.

There is a story about an old farmer who was sitting on his porch one day when a salesman came to call. As he stepped onto the porch, the salesman saw a pig in the front yard with only three legs. The fourth leg was wooden.

"Is that really a pig with a wooden leg?" the salesman asked.

"Yeah, it is," the farmer drawled.

"But how come that pig has a wooden leg?" inquired the salesman.

"Well, that's a right smart pig," answered the farmer. "I was down there plowing the field one day, and the tractor fell over and pinned me to the ground. I would have died, but that pig saw what happened and came over and dug me out from under the tractor. He saved my life."

"That's incredible," the astonished salesman replied. "But it doesn't explain why he has a wooden leg."

"You don't seem to understand, mister," continued the farmer. "I said that was a smart pig. One night we were all in the house asleep, and the house caught fire. We didn't even smell the smoke, my wife, my kids and me. That pig started snorting and squealing and making all kinds of noise, and we woke up and realized our house was on fire. The pig saved us and saved our house."

"That's the most amazing story I ever heard," said the salesman. "But you still haven't answered my question. Why does the pig have a wooden leg?"

The farmer replied, "Mister, you don't think that if we had a pig that smart we'd be stupid enough to eat him all at once!"

If any force is going to overcome a free, prosperous country like America, it won't happen all at once. America has a solid foundation of liberty, personal dignity, and opportunity. Anybody can rise above his social circumstances. There's no caste system. You don't have to be a member of the nobility to get ahead.

The only way to destroy something with that kind of foundation is to chip away at it, one value at a time. Take away its heart and essence. Bring doubt to what used to be confidence, denial to what used to be faith, death to what was life. I think that is what has happened.

Contrast the generation of the Great Depression with the generation of today. During the Depression, people were poor, hungry, and out of work. Yet they didn't engage in the kind of gang violence we have in schools today. Students weren't killing each other for a pair of shoes. Crime could easily have been justified by saying, "I'm hungry, and I don't have as much as you; therefore, I have a right to take what I can get." Dishonesty was still considered wrong, and thieves were despised.

Public officials and the policies they set show how far we have drifted, one tiny step at a time. When I was president of the Arkansas Baptist State Convention, Bill Clinton was governor. Clinton was experienced and savvy enough to recognize that the half-million Baptists in the state were probably the largest constituency he had. His antenna was attuned to that constituency, and from time to time he and I would discuss various issues.

During a heated discussion on abortion, Dr. Joycelyn Elders told Christians they needed to "get over their love affair with the fetus," an infamous phrase that was often repeated after she became surgeon general. The comment outraged even non-Christians, but particularly offended conservative believers. Governor Clinton called me and wanted to know how much of a problem this kind of comment was causing. I told him it was a serious problem. She had deeply offended many people. It was a slap in the face to those who held pro-life convictions.

"I wish you would explain to her how people in the evangelical world feel," he said. "Would you be willing to talk with her?"

I said I'd be happy to. So he set up a meeting and I went to visit her. We talked in her office for several hours. After we finished, I recognized she was absolutely sincere in her beliefs. I also realized that the reason her positions on these issues so conflicted with mine was that our worldviews were fundamentally at odds. Reaching a consensus was impossible. Like my son and his cake-baking experience, she had her own idea of what a "dash" of salt was—in this case a "dash" of human life—and recognized no fixed standard that could show her she was wrong.

We agreed there were problems with crime, poverty, disease, and other social ills. Where we disagreed was in identifying the source of the problems. She said they came from ignorance. She thought people needed to be educated and that we had a sexually transmitted disease problem because of a lack of education. Her solution therefore was sex education, drug education, and AIDS education in our schools. If we educated people about the risks of these types of behavior, they would avoid them. If we educated them in general knowledge—math, science, English, history—people would do better because they would know better. Then we could eliminate crime. In her view, our problems continue to plague us essentially because of economics: if we would only pour more money into education, education could wipe the slate clean.

★ ★ ★

Is Man Good?

Dr. Elders argued that man is basically good; therefore, if he does bad things, he simply doesn't realize they are bad, or else he hasn't been trained to do good. Her solution was to tell people, "This is a good way to live. You are really not a bad person; you just haven't found your goodness yet."

It sounds noble and, frankly, it seems a much more appealing approach to life than the alternative. It has but a single flaw: it's wrong. It will never work because our problems do not result from economics or deficiencies in education. They result from the selfish decision to ignore God's standards of integrity. Standards based on anything else are relative, and relative standards are meaningless.

A person with a biblical worldview says humans are by nature selfish. We are not basically good; rather, we are basically self-centered, look out for ourselves first, and preserve ourselves first at all costs. Only two things will change this behavior: either our nature will be changed by a supernatural experience with God through Christ, or we will fear the consequences of not doing the right thing. If we remove those consequences and make it easy to steal and lie with impunity, then we will do those things freely. We will do whatever brings us pleasure.

The biblical Book of Judges describes one of the darkest times in Old Testament history, and it uses one unforgettable line to explain the reason for the darkness: "Everyone did what was right in his own eyes" (21:25). That is precisely where we are today.

You hear it in our language. "If it feels good, do it." "What's in it for me?" Advertising slogans underscore the trend. "We do it all for you." "Have it your way." "You deserve a break today." "This Bud's for you." They all appeal to our basic, selfish nature—we are deserving and we are good.

Those who believe God created humans have a different worldview from those who believe humans created God. Are we here to have nature serve us, or are we here because we are to serve nature? Politics are totally directed by worldview. That's why when people say, "We ought to separate politics from religion," I say to separate the two is absolutely impossible.

★ ★ ★

When Man Becomes God

Public debate today is filled with arguments that, not long ago, would have been dismissed as ridiculous and insupportable. Consider homosexuality, for instance. There have been homosexuals in every human culture. But until recently, who would have dared to suggest that the practice should be accepted on equal footing with heterosexuality, to be thought of as a personal decision and nothing more?

Abortion also became OK because we decided it is OK. Where did we get the right to make that decision? Because we're our own god. If the inconvenience of this little child would interrupt our college education or a relationship with a boyfriend or girlfriend, then that child becomes nothing more than a choice. "It's my choice. I decide for myself. What about me?" That is the essence of our culture.

Everything you do and believe in is directed by your answer to the ultimate question: Is there a God? It all comes down to that single issue. If there is a God, then everything moves one way. If there isn't, it moves another.

The next question is this: If there is a God, can we know that God? If we can't know that God, then it doesn't matter whether He exists. But if we can know Him, that knowledge fundamentally directs our lives.

Subsequent questions naturally follow from this. If we can know Him, then how can we know Him? How does He reveal Himself to us? If we can know Him, and if He does reveal Himself, how does He relate to me? What does He expect of me? How am I accountable to Him? What happens if I am not accountable to Him? My whole life will be directed by the value I place on the answers to those questions.

On the other hand, if I believe that I somehow created God because I needed some explanation for the inexplicable; if I believe the only real world is the one I'm living in right now, and that when I die I will turn back to dust and that there isn't any more than that then I will live only for myself and only for the moment. God might have given me some sort of ability to cope with the perplexities of life. I might use Christian terms and practice some civil religion, but it doesn't substantially change my behavior because I don't really believe I will have to give account of my actions someday.

Everything comes down to the faith question, which then leads to the integrity question: Where does integrity of character come from? Either it comes from God or it comes from something we manufacture. If it comes from God, it is fixed. Of course, in practice we will invariably fall short of perfection, but our practice will always butt against a fixed absolute, the standard that is the same today, yesterday, and forever. The standard my grandfather had will be the same standard my grandchildren will have. We may pull away from it further and more often, but the standard stays.

If I don't believe there is a God, then I don't believe character is fixed. I believe it moves as the culture moves. Therefore, what was wrong once is no longer wrong because the culture no longer considers it inappropriate; we are able to move the standards. Proverbs 23:10 warns against moving "the ancient landmark" or boundary stone set by our forefathers. That means that once you move your reference point, everything else becomes chaos.

After the tornado devastated my state in 1997, I was visiting Arkadelphia. I had lived there when I was in college and that was where Janet and I first lived as a couple, so the town was familiar to me. But everything I remembered about the place had vanished. There was so much devastation that when I stood in the middle of town I could find no familiar reference points. Not a wall, not a sign. Nothing but piles of rubble for blocks and blocks.

Had there been one landmark—say, the hardware store—I could have identified everything else in town, even though it lay in ruins. Across the street, that pile of debris used to be a shoe store. Two blocks down, that twisted steel was a government office. But with no reference points, I was completely lost.

That is essentially what is happening to our society. We're lost because we recognize no fixed reference point. By refusing to define character using fixed standards, we lose our reference point, we lose our ability to navigate, and, therefore, we drift. Who is right and who is wrong? Who knows?

There is obviously a sense of order in the world. If there weren't, we wouldn't be here; there would only be a mass of molecules swirling around in the universe. Instead we have oak trees and rose blossoms and the delicate twists and turns of a newborn baby's ear. That order could only be directed and ordained by God. The same Master who fixed the seasons of the year and put the birds in the sky is the solid, unmoving reference point we must fix our lives on.

Does God exist? He has to, or we wouldn't exist ourselves.

X

Faith Is Like a Bass Boat

Our faith determines how we react to the culture in which we live. Because it so fundamentally defines us, we can't allow faith to take a secondary role in making day-to-day decisions.

I took a lot of heat as a candidate for "dirtying" my calling as a pastor. No one pretends that politics is pretty or clean. But that's why Christians need to get involved. The less salt and light there is in a place, the more beneficial the Christian point of view can be.

Christians can't refuse to get involved in an issue because it's messy; that's where they're needed most. Jesus didn't avoid the unwashed. He ministered to them. He even ate dinner with a tax collector! Christians need to pull on their hip boots and wade into the swamp of social and moral issues. It's hard to "rescue the perishing" if we're standing on the bank in freshly laundered clothes, refusing to get a little dirty.

I love to fish. Fortunately, fishing is one recreational activity I can still enjoy as governor. By myself or with members of my family, I can occasionally slip off to the Arkansas River for a couple of hours without causing a lot of commotion. (The other leisure activity I can still get away with is going to movies. Once I'm inside the theater and it's dark, my presence causes no disruption.)

From time to time I fish for trout in some of Arkansas's premier streams, but my favorite is bass fishing. I like the strategy and the challenge. I also enjoy the quiet and the chance to visit in a relaxed environment with Janet, the children, or some good friends. For my fortieth birthday, Janet surprised me with a fabulous bass boat—a metallic blue BassCat Pantera II with casting chairs, a 150-horsepower Mercury outboard, a fish finder, and even a stereo! The boat is parked in back of the governor's mansion so I can see it whenever I look out of the breakfast room windows.

Sitting there in the sunlight, its metallic paint sparkles, its controls and instruments glisten, and the trailer shines. Janet has great taste—that rig would be the envy of any true bass angler. But it looks pristine only as long as it's sitting in the driveway. To get any use out of it, I have to be willing to get it dirty.

I can imagine some proud fisherman who spends all day cleaning, waxing, and shining his boat. The ropes are perfectly coiled, the rods and tackle all neatly stored, the chrome without a single fingerprint. He trailers his rig to boat shows to meet other bass fishermen, also with beautiful rigs. They sit around and talk about how their boats perform—how comfortable the seats are, how roomy the bait lockers are, how fast the engines can get them to their favorite secret spot on the lake.

They might even put out a newsletter with articles about how to maintain the boats and keep them looking sharp, calendars of upcoming events, and point systems for improving their scores in boat show competitions.

But put those beautiful rigs in the water? Never! Imagine dulling that mirror finish, gained only after months of waxing. River water has sticks, leaves, algae, and goodness knows what else in it. There might even be old logs or stumps under the surface. Someone might spill gasoline in the boat. And think of all the muddy footprints! Yucky bait! Smelly, slimy fish flopping around!

These so-called "fishermen" end up with a beautiful boat, designed and built to do a specific job, which is absolutely useless out of the water. Unless they're willing to get it dirty, the boat is of no value.

★ ★ ★

Use Your Faith

Faith is like a bass boat. If we acquire it just to admire it, we might as well not have it at all. Just feeling self-satisfied with our faith isn't enough. We have to be willing to act on that feeling, to put our faith to the use for which it was meant. We can't stand around bemoaning the problems of the world, refusing to act because the situations or the people involved are disagreeable. Those should be the very situations that spur us on. The nastier the water, the more valuable it is to have a boat.

Being governor has led me to depend on faith with a new sense of urgency. I face situations every day that would be insurmountable without using the faith God has given me to make decisions.

Less than a month after I took office, I had to decide whether to sign the order for a convicted murderer to be executed. The night of an execution is the loneliest night of a governor's life. I had always favored the death penalty. I could speak about it freely, often gave speeches in favor of it, and even delivered sermons from the pulpit on the subject. I was quite comfortable defending it biblically as well as politically.

But there is a difference between abstract, hypothetical discussion and affixing your signature to set in motion the process by which a man will have his life terminated. I sat in the east conference room of the governor's mansion with an open line to the death chamber. Each step of the process was described to me. "They are bringing him into the death chamber now. They're strapping him to the gurney. . . ." For about two hours we kept an open line to see if there was any change from the Supreme Court or a stay from the federal court.

Finally the moment came when the warden got on the phone and said, "Governor, the prisoner is now prepared. The IV is inserted. Is there any reason we should not proceed?" What came out of my mouth in the next few moments would mean either the life or death of a man. I alone had the power to stop the proceedings or to say, "Proceed," and know that within four to twelve minutes, a human being would be dead.

I cannot describe what that is like. I could not have prepared myself for it. I have authorized four other executions since that one. It hasn't become any easier. I hope and pray it never does. If it does, there is something terribly wrong with me or the process.

I took my action with a sense of resolve, and to this day I am confident that I did the right thing—right defined against moral absolutes in the midst of an imperfect world.

In an ideal world, this man would never have committed the horrible murders for which he was tried and found guilty. The process was both tedious and thorough. He had every opportunity to appeal. He was found guilty and sentenced to die. Nevertheless, the moment a governor gives the order to proceed, he is answering to God for his action and not to the taxpayers.

✶   ✶   ✶

Thank God for Absolutes

At those critical moments in my life, I thank God for His absolutes. I don't see how anyone could go about making decisions otherwise. I've heard spirited debates on the subject and find that those arguing against the existence of absolutes have never thought through the logical consequences of their position.

If there are no absolutes—if nothing can be defined as either always right or always wrong—then there must be no God. As one philosopher has said, "If there is no God, then everything is permitted." But if there is a God, there are absolutes.

If there is no God and no absolutes, then nothing is always right and nothing is always wrong. Right and wrong can only be determined by what a majority of the people believe and accept at a certain time and in a certain place, and so it is (in the purest sense) a system in which the majority rules. Whatever the people consent to becomes "right."

If there are no moral absolutes, then the United States had no right to intervene and tell the Third Reich that the annihilation of

Jews was wrong. After all, if there are no absolutes, then the majority rules—and by definition, their decision must be right. "But," people may argue, "we all know that is wrong." But how do we all know any such thing? How can something be wrong if the majority assents to it and has the power to enforce it? In such cases, the logic of relativism disappears. No one can live for long with a system that disallows God and disallows moral absolutes because no one can live with the consequences if they follow relativism to its natural conclusion.

Or consider another example. Why do we care about victims of natural disasters? After all, it wasn't our house that was destroyed. Answer: Because we "feel something."

And why do we "feel something"? Is it social pressure? If so, we can shake that off. Or do we "feel something" because we have a conscience? And if we have a conscience, where did it come from? Where does the moral compass come from that makes us want to show compassion, to give of ourselves, to believe there is something better?

Relativism is an enormous stumbling block to the governments of atheistic countries. I once heard that the Chinese ambassador to the United Nations accused America of trying to impose its human rights standards unfairly on the Chinese people. He said Chinese standards were different, and he's right. "Chinese standards" of human rights have caused unimaginable death and suffering through the years. Adherence to God's immovable standard in that nation would result in new hope and new opportunities for more than a billion of the world's people. But where there are no absolutes, the leadership is free to set whatever standards it likes.

★ ★ ★

The Consequences of Drifting

Everyone has friends who have faced harsh consequences as a result of drifting from their moral center. Dick Morris conducted opinion polls for me when I was lieutenant governor. I found him to be a fascinating individual. We could hardly be more different. He's a classic New Yorker, raised in Manhattan, the son of a prominent attorney. I was born in Hope, Arkansas. My father was a fireman, and I went to a small Baptist university.

As a person to track public opinion, he was ideal. Someone who thinks and acts the same way I do will only reinforce my own opinions. In a political campaign, Dick could test all of our political ideas and policy positions. You don't really know if your position is defensible until you know you can sell it to people who are not like you. In politics, it's tempting to surround yourself with people who think the same way you do, but that can be dangerous. On the other hand, you don't want to surround yourself with people who can manipulate you. Dick could be dangerous to a person who didn't know what he believed. If you weren't secure in your convictions, he could soon have you believing what he believed.

We had a lot of arguments, but I learned a great deal from him about how to shape and communicate my ideas. He is a brilliant political strategist.

Yet the whole country learned that Dick was having an extramarital affair. How could it have happened? In my view, it was the result of his never embracing a moral center. He had no fixed reference point, no immovable absolute. He substituted his own standards of relative morality for true morality, and the result came back to haunt him.

Whether it's in public policy or with friends, Christians have opportunities every day to put their faith to work. Take your faith off the trailer and head out into the murky waters of daily obstacles and challenges. That's what it was built for.

XI

Decisions, Decisions

As governor, I spend a large part of my day making decisions about issues that affect other people's lives. I even have to make decisions about which decisions to make.

The first step is to separate the immediate from the ultimate. Everybody's needs are immediate, but they aren't all ultimate. Everyone believes his or her needs are the most important things in the world. The tough part of my job is having to decide in what part of the food chain a particular issue lies. Usually it isn't anywhere close to where the parties involved think it is. When I make a decision based on such a judgment, people are bound to be disappointed. But the job requires it.

Next, I ask how great an impact the issue will have. How many people are involved? How wide an area is affected? How much money is involved? Does it have long-term consequences? If you tell me there's a bird about to be killed outside, I know that if the bird dies, it dies, and that's that. But if you tell me there's a disease out there that could affect every bird that flies, that is more important. I have to examine the facts and decide if it's an isolated incident or an ongoing problem. Is it an avalanche rolling down the side of the mountain, or is it a single snowball that's already been thrown and has melted? I have to separate the big from the small.

Dr. Vester Wolber was a professor of religion when I attended Ouachita and was one of the wisest people I have ever met. He had a lot of little sayings, one of which was, "Don't use all your water to put out too small a fire." Sometimes we overreact to something others perceive as a crisis and use all the water we have to put out a small fire. Then when the bigger ones come, we have no resources left. That kind of temptation can get someone in my position in trouble. If you allow them to, persuasive, well-meaning people will drain every ounce of energy you have for something that doesn't deserve it. I have to say no constantly.

I have a staffer in charge of handling problems in our 311 school districts. When she finds one, getting it solved is the most important issue of the day. But I have hundreds of boards and agencies, 53,000 employees, and 2.5 million bosses. And the other 310 school districts have problems too. Sometimes I have to say, "I understand your concern and I appreciate your work, but I have other concerns as well. That is why I am not going to spend three hours talking to that third-grade teacher." It's not that I don't care, but I don't have three hours to give to it. Making a call like that is part of the job. I use my lists to decide which issue to consider next.

Another saying I like is that "the difference between successful people and failures is that successful people are willing to do the things failures don't like to do." When you make your list, if you go back and pick out the things that aren't pleasant and do them first, you'll get a lot more done. Most people do the opposite. They take care of tasks they enjoy first, make sure the fun stuff takes up all their time, and leave the rest of their tasks undone. Then they rationalize by saying, "I was going to do these things, but I ran out of time." It's like the child who tries to get out of cleaning his room by saying there was an educational program on TV he "had to watch."

Another goal is to make "duty" decisions only once. If you say, "I'm going to join a church," then don't wake up Sunday morning and spend thirty minutes debating whether you're going. Don't waste time dealing with decisions you've already made. If you say, "I'm going to abstain from sex until I get married," then don't struggle with that every time you go on a date. You've already decided that, and it's now your duty.

★ ★ ★

How to Choose Employees

When considering someone for a job, make sure that person has mastered his current level of responsibility before giving him more. There's always someone who says, "I really need to be a department director. I can manage something bigger. I'm not really fulfilled where I am." If you aren't able to do well where you start, you will probably never go beyond where you start. In fact, you'll probably go below that level.

People who are uncomfortable where they are will not become more comfortable after they get where they want to go. If a person can't be content starting at the bottom, he won't be content at the top. It doesn't matter where you are in the pecking order because your contentment doesn't come from there. It comes from the internal confidence that wherever you are, you're growing and building on your experience to the best of your ability within that system.

Beware of people who judge themselves on the basis of how well somebody else does. Our goal should be to do the best we can. Then we won't begrudge people who are doing better than we are. Nor will we fear that we will be left behind. We're never left behind unless we are worried about being on someone else's track. God has a unique track for all of us. We don't have to run like someone else; we're not supposed to.

★ ★ ★

How to Settle an Argument

One real challenge is deciding how to settle an argument when both sides have made a good effort to agree, yet have failed to find a compromise and have given up and dug in their heels. The wheels of government can't grind to a halt because two people can't find common ground.

The pathway to resolving what seems to be an irreconcilable disagreement starts with finding out what each party really wants. Often this approach will untangle even the messiest impasse in minutes. Although the two sides think they know what they want, and they may say what they think they want, deep down it may be something else. This is true in marriage, business, and politics. What does each side really want, and what do they need? The need may be different from their stated goals. It may be that their argument is indefensible, but human nature is such that no one ever wants to say, "That was a really stupid idea I've been chasing these past few months."

The solution may be to suggest a graceful way out without the appearance of having suffered a defeat, so that the buyer goes his way saying, "I got it for a low price," while the seller says, "I sold it for a high price," and everyone goes away with what he wanted. The goal is to have both parties thinking they have won.

Most people don't even know what their basic needs are. Suppose that in a marriage a husband and wife are fighting over money. It's probably not a matter of money; it's an issue of control. It might also be an issue of fear. If the husband grew up not having much money, it may be a fear of returning to poverty. If the wife grew up having a lot of money and then lost it and earned it back, she might be thinking, *Easy come, easy go.*

You need to give each person some confidence in the matter. Make sure that one knows everything is going to be OK: the risk does not mean bankruptcy. At the same time, assure the other that there will be opportunities for risk while still saving money. Once you can determine the real issue, you can work toward a solution in which both parties can feel they've won—not over the other party, but over their own struggles and doubts.

★ ★ ★

Solving the Unsolvable

While most problems have a solution, some don't. In those cases, you have to be willing to choose your side, confront your opponents, and hold tight to your position. If you get beat, go down swinging, but absolutely refuse to cave in.

We fought a battle in the legislature regarding a ban on partial birth abortions. We made it clear: we may lose, but we will never back down. We ultimately won the battle and passed legislation to prohibit this gruesome procedure in Arkansas.

In another piece of state legislation, the General Assembly wanted to control capital improvements budget and started buying off legislators left and right. I stated throughout, "You may beat us, but you won't buy us." This time we lost, but nobody bought us. There are some lines you cannot cross. Make them clear, and stand firm.

Caution is important because once you take that sort of stand, there's more at stake than just the issue. Your character is on the line too. If you cave in, your credibility will be instantly and permanently gone. No one will trust you again. So make sure the issue is worth going to the wall for.

It all goes back to desire versus duty. We have a duty to accomplish certain things: to uphold the Constitution and to be right and honorable. On the other hand, the desire might be, "I would like to have this office space, this staff, or this function." No one is going to perish if he doesn't satisfy his desire. But he might if you don't fulfill your duty.

★ ★ ★

No Compromise on Core Convictions

Every decision has consequences. Whatever you do, never compromise your core convictions. I find myself encouraged to compromise every day. You have to know your limits. What line can you absolutely not cross? What level can you absolutely not go beyond? Know what these are, and stick to them.

The applications of this principle are endless, but one example comes to mind. As governor, people are always telling me they are my friends and want to help. They come with the idea that "I need you to do this for me because I am doing that for you." The easiest trap in the world is to begin to renegotiate your principles just a little bit to pay back a friend or to do something nice for someone who has done something nice for you.

There may be people who are doing things for you with pure motives, but you can never allow yourself to fall into the trap of letting their favors influence your decisions. If you ever let that guard down, you'll be in real trouble. You can be grateful to get what proper favors you receive. But never think for a moment you would have gotten them had you not been governor. Or that you will get them after you leave. You won't.

Some of what I know about making decisions comes from experience, but I hope most of it comes as spiritual wisdom from God. If there is one example I can offer about decision making, it's in my daily reading from Proverbs and my study of the Sermon on the Mount. I have always said that if a person had nothing to read but the Sermon on the Mount and the Book of Proverbs, he would have a more credible basis for management than any book ever written on the subject. I have never been exposed to a principle of good management that I couldn't find in the Sermon on the Mount or the Book of Proverbs. They cut to the heart of how to become a successful manager and why to do it.

My philosophy of life is to take God very seriously, but never to take myself very seriously. Fear God, honor Him, love Him, worship Him, and always remember He is the standard. He is personified in Jesus Christ; therefore, whatever He says He is, we take that seriously. On the other hand, I do not take myself too seriously. I can't afford to feel self-important or indispensable. Other people have been governor of Arkansas and more will follow after I'm gone. There isn't a job in this world somebody else hasn't done, will do, and probably will do better. I could compare myself to others, but that is not my standard. My standard is Christ; I will have to answer to Him alone.

⋆ ⋆ ⋆

The Necessity of Fun

Of course, taking Christ seriously doesn't mean you can't have fun. You must have a sense of humor as governor. You have to blow off some steam. It's tragic that some people are so afraid of enjoying life. To me, humor is a defense. I've read that many comedians are people in deep pain. They often are depressed; they are sometimes lonely and extraordinarily sensitive. Comedy becomes their defense mechanism. It's a way to release tension, relieve their burdens, and shake off depression.

When Norman Mailer had cancer, he went on "humor therapy." He wrote an article called "I Laughed Myself to Health." Scientists now know that laughter releases endorphins into the body, natural pain relievers with almost the same effect as a narcotic.

There is real power in having a sense of humor. Proverbs 17:22 says, "A merry heart doeth good like a medicine, but their bitter spirit dries up the bones." Sometimes the best medicine we can reach for is not a bottle or a pill, but a joke book. The capacity to laugh, to make light of situations that are heavy, is incredibly important. Morticians have their own brand of death humor. Soldiers have their combat humor. They must have that to survive. If you go into your job thinking the whole world is on your shoulders—if you feel that kind of unbearable pressure—you need to release it in some way. And humor is a great way to do it.

☆ ☆ ☆

The Necessity of Inner Peace

In everything I do, I need to be at peace with myself. If my world were to come crashing down, I don't want to say, "That's the end of everything!" Nothing is more important to me than having peace with myself as a Christian, being in Jesus Christ, and knowing that whatever I do, the potential of grace and forgiveness is there. That doesn't give me license for a life of carelessness! It gives me a sense of direction.

Our goal as Christians is to please Him, to emulate Him. We don't want to displease Him, to try and get away with as much as possible. That would show indifference toward Jesus and disrespect for God, and a person who acts that way clearly doesn't know God.

I'm sure about one thing: I not only want to know Him, I want others to be able to see Him through the decisions I make and by the way I make them.

XII

* * *

A   M e d i u m   R a r e l y

W e l l   D o n e

I am not afraid of television. I was doing television by age twenty-one and began hosting my first TV show on our church station in Pine Bluff in 1984. Television is the most powerful tool in history for reaching a large audience, and anyone who expects to shape public policy these days has to be comfortable in front of a camera.

That is not necessarily comforting news to intelligent, capable politicians who despise being on television—but television is the medium of the moment in America. Many people in the public eye forge ahead with their plans, ignoring the power of television, and then wonder why no one understands or supports their ideas. Even public figures who successfully withstand television's unblinking gaze often don't make the most of its potential to help them.

Television was an indispensable ally for me on July 15, 1996, when I was able to speak to the whole state and tell Arkansans what was happening with the Jim Guy Tucker debacle. I believe the electronic media are neutral rather than automatically hostile. Television is like fire. Fire can be good or it can be bad. It can burn you, but it also can warm you, cook your food, and purify.

★ ★ ★

How to Manage the Media

Several points are helpful in dealing with the media. One is not to be afraid. Whether you like it or not, the media provide the vehicle through which whatever you do or say is delivered to people. I have to accept the reality that Arkansans' perceptions of me and what I am doing come through the media.

Second, you must diversify your contacts with various types of media. Never have one reporter or one newspaper be your only contact. Don't become dependent on one medium, either. Some public officials say they want to deal only with television, radio, newspapers, cable, or whatever. That's a mistake; all of them are important.

Today's diversity of media is a great benefit. It used to be that there were a limited number of media you could use to help you project a public image: newspaper, radio, or TV. Now there are new technologies like the Internet. There are newsletters, magazines, trade journals—many ways to communicate a message—and you need to take advantage of them all. If a newspaper doesn't like you, there may be nothing you can do to change that. You have to be ready to counter it with other information outlets.

I doubt there is a politician alive who hasn't had a run-in with a reporter who simply doesn't like him and will always write things with a negative slant. You can't stop such biased reporting, but you can try to circumvent it by finding enough honest reporters to balance those slanted reports.

★ ★ ★

The Power of Television

There is no question that television has totally changed politics. In fact, I wonder if a man as homely as Lincoln or as big as Taft could be elected president in the television age. I'm sometimes criticized because I use TV and radio frequently. (I have monthly radio and TV programs now as governor, so anyone in the state can speak directly with me about concerns he has.) Political opponents accuse me of glossing over the issues and say it's "not fair" that I am relaxed and believable on the air. Style shouldn't count, they say.

First of all, style alone has never gotten anybody elected. Second, if the people want to elect a bumbling idiot who can't put a sentence together and appears incredibly nervous on camera, there's nothing to stop them from it. But don't dismiss someone just because he's comfortable talking to people through our society's most effective medium of communication. Such an attitude is like getting mad at someone because he runs the mile faster than you, when running fast is the whole point! If the medium of winning the race is the track, then learn to run on that track. If you're going to be in a football game, learn to grab the ball, hold onto it, and get it to the goal line. If the medium for moving public policy is television, then understand that TV is the field of play and learn to run on it. Don't complain about it. Accept the facts for what they are.

It doesn't mean you have to give up your intellect; it means you have to be able to demonstrate that intellect in the medium the public has chosen. If you can't do that, then you probably aren't going to be successful in politics today.

XIII

★ ★ ★

C a n d i d a t e

i n   t h e   M i r r o r

Although President Bill Clinton and I obviously differ greatly on political issues, in many ways the president represents what Republicans promote in their public policy: self-determination, setting goals, and overcoming adversity on your own.

Young Bill Clinton was poor and disadvantaged; but from the time he was young, he was focused like a laser on becoming president of the United States. It's what he wanted; it's what he worked for and sacrificed for, and through the years he managed to remove all the barriers to his goal. While there are 260 million Americans who can say whatever they want about him, he'll sleep in the White House tonight and the rest of us won't. In that way, Bill Clinton's rise to success epitomizes the American dream.

★ ★ ★

"But You Know, I Like Him"

Bill Clinton overcame more than his humble upbringing to become president. The year before the 1992 election, President Bush's approval ratings were through the roof as a result of the Persian Gulf War. Meanwhile, Clinton had to face accusations of extramarital activity, experimental drug use, and even a question of his patriotism during the Vietnam War. His policies on issues such as homosexuality and abortion were anathema to the mainstream evangelical community.

And yet, when it came to making a decision, American voters ended up saying, "But you know, I like him." People were more interested that someone reflect who they were rather than someone they wanted to be or thought they should be. When voters got up in the morning and looked in the mirror, they didn't see fighter pilot, CIA director, China envoy, President Bush. That made them uncomfortable. They were more like that young, flawed, sincere man Bill Clinton.

★ ★ ★

A Watershed Year

This sort of thinking—*the president is just like me*—is the gradual result of post-Watergate cynicism. The Nixon administration was vilified because back then we had an idealistic image of a president; we wanted him to be the most honorable, most statesmanlike of all of us. He represented more than himself. He represented all that was good about our country. We wanted our political leaders to be statesmen and we thought of them in those terms.

But in the post-Watergate era, cynicism mushroomed. People started not only accepting the worst, but *expecting* the worst from their elected officials.

I became a teenager in 1968, a year I have always considered a watershed date in American history. That year marked the death of innocence: the assassinations of Robert Kennedy and Martin Luther King Jr., the Chicago riots, and the horror of Vietnam. The world didn't change completely in a single year, but in 1968 the shift in our society became too apparent to miss. People were angry. Student protests and the hippie movement were at fever pitch. The Black Panthers came into their own. There was a total loss not just of innocence, but of a sense of community and wholesomeness. It really did mark a turning point. From that year onward, we have lived in the age of the birth control pill, free love, gay sex, the drug culture, and reckless disregard for standards.

The turn-on-tune-in-drop-out movement gave personal debauchery a new license. People felt free to do whatever they wanted. Your norm and my norm became the cultural norm. No longer did we live by the standards of God; it became, "You define your standard, I'll define mine, and everybody will be happy. Nobody can tell me to pray; nobody can tell me to read a Bible; nobody can tell me what is right and wrong. I have to make those decisions for myself." It was the beginning of the Me Generation, which mushroomed in the seventies. By the time we got to Watergate, morality had become a joke.

★ ★ ★

Should We Talk about It?

Not long ago, no reporter would consider running an exposé on the president's personal life. Indiscretion was considered horrendous. You just didn't talk about those things in public. Respect for the office and a sense of public decorum prevented it.

Back in the 1920s President Warren G. Harding had numerous mistresses, one of whom bore him a child—but it never hit the front-page news. We thought then that our presidents were better than that. When Franklin Roosevelt died, he was on vacation with a woman other than his wife, a woman he had promised he would not see again. Yet the scandal mill produced no grist. During the sixties, it would have been unthinkable for anyone to publish news of President Kennedy's intimate White House escapades, or run a photo of Jackie—a heavy smoker—with a Marlboro hanging from her lip. Both public figures and the media were discreet, even about indiscretions.

As forces chipped away at American morality, people became increasingly bold about their lifestyles. Gays proudly came out of the closet. Pushers and users openly discussed drugs and drug addiction. Movie stars all but bragged on television about their affairs and their bouts with alcohol. Divorce lost any kind of stigma as did teen pregnancy.

And what role do the media play in this downward spiral? I believe the media only reflect culture; they don't create it. That is one place where I differ from many of my evangelical brothers. The media aren't a light, but a mirror. People buy what they see in themselves. That helps explain why in 1992 we elected Bill Clinton as president, not George Bush.

★ ★ ★

Pursuing the American Dream

My purpose in providing this kind of cultural critique is not to depress or anger you, but to urge you to become all you can be for the welfare of our country and for the glory of God. Pursuing such a goal won't be easy in our current culture, but it is possible. President Clinton and I are from the same hometown. We were both born in Hope, Arkansas. We went to the same kindergarten—Miss Marie's—nine years apart, then both attended Brookwood Elementary.

Even though we were born in the same town, we grew up in very different environments. The president has told the story of how he grew up with an abusive, alcoholic stepfather. I was fortunate to grow up without that sort of family tension. My father was a fireman who ran a little machine shop on weekends; my mother was a clerk.

Clinton went to college out of state, then on to England as a Rhodes Scholar. He had a secular educational environment. I went to Ouachita Baptist University, where I came to intellectual grips with my convictions and became comfortable with them beyond my emotions.

Today the president and I have a cordial, genuinely engaging relationship. He is warm, hospitable, and encouraging to everyone around him. That's one of the reasons he has been so successful. He can make anyone, regardless of who he or she is, feel comfortable and at home. He really enjoys being around people. I admire what he has been able to accomplish.

Of course, this doesn't mean I celebrate that the president's worldview is governing America—just the opposite. I think a lot of his decisions on partial birth abortions, social programs, and other issues are way off the mark. But there are two ways for us to approach the situation. One is to be angry and bitter that he is president. The other is to say, "If he could become president with his disadvantaged background, how many other young Americans could too?" Let's hope we train some of them to want the same goal.

I honestly hope Clinton's story will inspire others to become leaders, even if they start out in modest circumstances. People can look down on you for being poor or for other reasons, but you don't have to let it get to you. I know what it is like to be left behind, left out, or be the last one picked. I've been there. (Remember, I'm an Arkansas Republican.) When those sorts of painful things happen, you can either turn inward and retreat or rise above it, look beyond it, and believe in yourself. You have no control over where you start in life, but you do have control over where you finish.

I see kids visit the capitol all the time, just like I did when I first came on a fifth-grade field trip. They walk around, looking up at the high ceilings, eyes open wide. It might as well be the Taj Mahal. It is a beautiful building. The first time, it's an awesome sight. Children will say things to me like, "Are you really the governor?" or "Would you sign my book?" And I think, *Someday, you could be sitting in this office.*

My favorite time of day is when legislative pages come in to get their pictures taken or when I meet with school groups. I always try to encourage them. Most people think it would be boring to jump from one end of the room to the other for pictures, to stand near the flag, or to give a walk-through of the governor's office. But during these times I'm not so much looking at the cameras as I am the kids' faces and seeing how they respond to being there. Looking at it through their eyes makes me feel like a kid again. It really excites me. When I walked in as a fifth-grader, I never imagined that one day other fifth-graders would be coming to see *me* in that room.

With that in mind, it's my sincere hope that our culture's moral decline (as reflected in the media) does not discourage bright, young minds from pursuing the American dream. Rather, I hope that the great needs of this country will inspire our kids to become reformers, crusaders, leaders, governors—even presidents.

I know at least two little boys from Hope, Arkansas, who have found that to be true.

XIV

L e t   I t   S h i n e

I hear one comment a lot these days: "Now that you're governor, I guess you want to be the next guy from Arkansas to go to the White House."

If I really wanted to move up to the next level, I'd have plenty of company. There are 135 people in the legislature who think they could be governor. There are probably 50 governors who think they could be president; there are 100 senators and 435 members of the House who think the same thing. Wherever you are, there's a temptation to want to jump to the next level.

I have come to realize that my next position might be at quite a different level. It may be running a soup kitchen somewhere. I'd rather be doing something I know I'm supposed to do than something everybody tells me is right. If you're the governor of a state, there aren't many jobs you can take in that state that people will think are more important.

The great, liberating comfort for me and other believers is that God, not man, is in control, and He knows what is best for me. I am not to be so ambitious that I start thinking I know better than God what's best for me. That's not to say ambition is bad; everybody should have some ambition and strive to do his best. But I could run a marina and tackle shop at Lake Greeson near Murfreesboro and be quite content.

★ ★ ★

Following God's Lead

I've enjoyed doing everything I have ever done. I enjoyed pastoring a small church, serving as director of communications for a Christian ministry, and doing advertising, public relations, and promotional work. I enjoyed pastoring a church that grew from a small, struggling group to a large congregation.

Still, being governor of Arkansas is the most fulfilling, challenging, satisfying, and wonderful job I've had. I wouldn't trade the experience for anything. On the other hand, it doesn't make me any happier or make me feel any more important than when I was twenty-five years old and pastoring a struggling church in a declining neighborhood. I don't feel any better living in the governor's mansion than I did living in a forty-dollars-a-month duplex with Janet when we were married as eighteen-year-old college students. We were just as happy in a lot of ways.

Certainly my surroundings today are more attractive than they were then. Now I'm exposed to Persian rugs and fine pieces of art on loan from the Arkansas Arts Center. Somebody shines my shoes every night; I just set them outside the bedroom door. My clothes are freshly pressed; my meals are prepared; the beds are made; and other people place my phone calls and drive me to work. It's all quite convenient, and I appreciate it. But I was just as happy without it.

I think that is the ultimate joy. Like the apostle Paul, I can rejoice because I have seen both plenty and want. They're both interesting, and I can learn a lot from both positions. Persian rugs are nice, but I've been at the bottom too. I know firsthand that life is good even down there.

Though I've been happy in all of my careers, I freely admit I love the excitement of campaigning. It's the thrill of the unknown. The frantic pace. Some of us are crazy enough to enjoy it; others see it as a necessary evil. George Bush had great disdain for campaigning. Bill Clinton, on the other hand, is in my same camp in this regard. We both like people, and in campaigning the ultimate goal is to be with people—to share your views, listen, sympathize, and persuade. There's also the sense that you always have to be at a peak performance level. You never know when you'll slip. Anybody who campaigns with the assumption that the election is in the bag is living dangerously.

My years in the pastorate and in politics have reinforced my conviction that the most destructive forces in the world are not "out there" somewhere, but inside our hearts. By the same token, the most constructive forces in the world are not out there; they're internal. It always comes back to the fact that character is the most constructive force in the world.

Anyone in a position of responsibility can be eaten up with doubts and second-guessing. His weakness can cause him to accept bad advice with devastating results. But if you have integrity of character, you never have to second-guess, never have to feel guilty, never have to avoid looking people in the eye. The worst thing you can do is lose, and even then you can do so with honor.

On the other hand, if you don't embrace integrity of character, if you can't be at peace with yourself, if you are constantly at war with your soul and you have never resolved who you really are or what you believe in, then you can overcome every problem in the world, but you will only be dishonored and miserable in the end.

★ ★ ★

Only One Will Prevail

I see a growing polarization in our society. Sometimes it appears as though we are moving toward a more virtuous culture; at other times I'd swear we are moving toward utter chaos. I see this polarization in politics, the arts, business, education. People are beginning to move worlds apart and find it increasingly difficult to establish common ground.

Two opposing worldviews account for this polarization. One puts man at the center; the other puts God at the center. The two are absolutely *irreconcilable*. Consensus cannot be reached because the two sides do not even have a basis of agreement with which to begin a discussion.

One of the biggest faults of modern Christians is trying to reconcile a self-centered worldview with Christianity. It is impossible. I see people on one side who have deep Christian convictions; they will become more focused on character. Those on the other side will move steadily toward self-satisfaction.

The two major political parties in America have become polarized as well. Years ago it was a difficult task to pin down the ideological differences between a Republican and a Democrat in Arkansas. There were liberal Republicans and conservative Democrats, especially in the South. Party labels had more to do with social standing than ideology. That's no longer the case. You will now find very wealthy and very poor in both parties, and a distinct ideological separation.

Here's the bottom line not just for Arkansas and America, but for the world: one worldview will prevail. Either by numbers or persuasion, one side of this polarized culture will defeat the other in setting public policy. When two irreconcilable views emerge, one is going to dominate. Ours will either be a worldview with humans at the center or with God at the center. Standards of right and wrong are either what we establish as human beings (standards which can be changed to suit us), or they are what God has set in motion since the creation of the world and cannot be moved.

This clash is going to occur between those who think man is basically good (if he has enough education and economic parity with his brother, he will do good things and avoid crime, poverty, and disease), and those who say man is basically self-centered (he'll do whatever he can get away with unless his nature is changed by a supernatural act of God, or he is so shamed by the consequences of doing wrong that he is constrained to do right). The winning worldview will dominate public policy, the laws we make, and every other detail of our existence.

For example, if I believe man is basically good, then when I see that we have a high rate of teen pregnancy I will think, *If only people had education and economic parity, it wouldn't happen. I'll create a program that brings sex education to young women and young men, and make provisions for birth control. I'm going to spend money and provide education to the people.*

On the other hand, if I believe man is basically self-centered, then I'm going to create consequences for those actions. Instead of saying, "We're going to give you a book" or "We're going to give you a check," I'm going to say, "If you get pregnant, you are going to have a child to care for and support. You aren't going to live as comfortable a life."

How can we change a drug-addicted culture? Do we say, "If these people weren't poor, or if they only knew what drugs did, then they wouldn't be doing this"? If so, you'd prepare a bunch of informational videos and explain the danger. And in fact, that is just what much of government has been doing. And has it worked? No. Will it ever work? No. Why not? Because taking drugs appeals to the self-centered, pleasure-seeking people we are by nature.

If we're convinced of that selfish nature, we take a different tack: "If you use drugs, we're going to put you in jail for so long you won't even remember where you live. We are going to confiscate drugs. We're going to take your car, and if we catch you dealing, we're going to try you and convict you and take your liberty away."

We must come to see that our core problem is not lack of education but lack of righteousness. We don't need more information as much as we need new hearts.

Welfare, abortion, sexually transmitted diseases—every public issue is going to be approached differently depending on which worldview wins out. We aren't talking about degrees of difference; we're talking about one or the other with no ground in between. When I hear people say, "I don't think Christians (or "pastors" or "Baptists" or whatever) ought to get into politics," I respond, "If the Christian worldview does not prevail, the public policy that will teach your children and grandchildren—the policy that will rule their society as well as yours—will be formed by people who think your beliefs fell off the edge of the flat earth. They will defame what you respect and discount your reason for believing it. They will dismiss with rancor everything you think is important."

Is that what you're willing to settle for?

It's not that we want to impose our religion on somebody. It's that we want to shape the culture and laws by using a worldview we believe has value. Both sides believe in their position, but both can't be right.

★ ★ ★

A Candle in the Darkness

Can you make a difference in the battle between a God-centered worldview and a human-centered one? Can your little sputtering light of God-focused character do anything against the looming darkness of a lost world?

I learned the answer the summer before my senior year in high school. That year I went to Expo '72, the first worldwide evangelism conference staged by Campus Crusade for Christ. On the last night of the conference, Billy Graham spoke to almost one hundred thousand young people from all over the world in the Cotton Bowl in Dallas. His message was, "You can touch the world. One person can make a difference."

At the end of his message, the stadium lights went out, and the whole place went black. I was sitting at the other end of the stadium from Rev. Graham. Even at such a distance, with that vast darkness all around, I could see when he lit his candle. One tiny match brought the whole stadium from darkness into light. Graham used his candle to light another held by Bill Bright, the founder of Campus Crusade. The two men lit two other people's candles, making four candles in all; they each lit another candle, making eight.

Everyone in the stadium had been given a candle. As the people up front lit the candles of eight people in the audience, the light spread exponentially. Within a few minutes, one hundred thousand candles, all taking their light from that one candle in Billy Graham's hand, were so bright that people were calling the Dallas Fire Department and reporting the Cotton Bowl on fire. It was an incredible sight. And I realized, more than anything, that the darker things are, the more difference even the tiniest light will make.

Across the room from me there's a night light that stays plugged in all the time. I can't see it now. But if I were to turn off all the lights in this room, your eyes would focus on that little light. The darker it is in here, the more brilliant that tiny bulb will seem. It will penetrate the darkness. The darkness, no matter how great, can never swallow even the smallest light. All the darkness in the Cotton Bowl couldn't quench a single match.

Your spiritual light—your light of integrity, character, and a God-centered worldview—is just as invincible. We live in a dark spiritual age—all the more reason for you to hold your candle high and hold it out to others! The darker the world gets, the brighter your light will shine.

APPENDIXES:
SELECTED SPEECHES
AND COMMENTARY

Appendix 1

★ ★ ★

The Speech
That Never Was

This speech was prepared by Lieutenant Governor Huckabee to be delivered on a statewide television broadcast after his inauguration as governor of Arkansas on July 15, 1996. He had just finished rehearsing it when Governor Jim Guy Tucker called to say he had decided not to resign.

At two o'clock this afternoon, I took the oath of office to become your governor. The responsibility that has been thrust upon me and entrusted to me is one that I approach with unapologetic dependence upon the Spirit of God to give me the heart of a servant, wisdom for the difficult decisions I will face each day, the courage to stand by my convictions, and the humility to acknowledge my mistakes, of which there will be many.

A few weeks ago, when a jury of our fellow Arkansans patiently reached a verdict in a nearby federal courthouse, our state was shattered emotionally and politically. My decision to withdraw from the race for the United States Senate and concentrate wholeheartedly on serving as your governor is one I do not regret. I want to help restore Arkansas's image to America as a place of natural beauty, hard-working people, and a family-friendly atmosphere. . . .

While so much attention is focused upon us, I ask every fellow Arkansan to join me in ensuring that America and the world come to know the Arkansas we know and love. Let's make sure the nation sees our real strengths: Nature. Family. Community. We're the kind of folks who take food to a sick friend, put an arm around the shoulder of one who grieves, and who speak a sincere and friendly greeting to those we meet.

Our transition team has been nothing short of amazing during the past seven weeks. With limited resources and time, literally hundreds of Arkansas citizens volunteered and came aboard to help make sure that the people's business would be treated with care. My deepest thanks and utmost praise go to everyone who has worked to prepare for a new beginning in Arkansas.

You may want to know more about your new first family. Janet, my wife of 22 years, has been the love of my life since our senior year of high school in our hometown of Hope. You may end up not caring much for me, but you're going to love your first lady. She's a great wife and mother, but most of all she's a most unpretentious person who can charm guests at a formal reception but is just as comfortable shooting basketball with a high school team, bungee jumping, or making snow cones in a

PTA concession booth. We have three teenage children, and that's reason enough to be patient with us. Our oldest son, John Mark, will be a sophomore at Ouachita Baptist University this fall. David is 16, and Sarah turns 14 this summer, and we'll be enrolling both of them in the Little Rock public school system as soon as we get settled.

You're entitled to ask, "What kind of governor will you be?" I plan to be guided by certain principles that will form the basis of policies enabling *every* Arkansas citizen to claim our state truly as the "Land of Opportunity."

1. Those of us elected or employed to serve the citizens need to remember who the boss is. The people who walk through our doors or who call us on our phones are not "nuisances," "irritations," or even "customers." We need to treat them like the boss because we work for them. They pay for the government we give them. And the owners have a right to be treated with dignity, courtesy, and efficiency. Government was created to serve its people; its people were not created to serve government.

A few weeks ago a reporter cynically asked, "What qualifications or credentials do these so-called volunteers on your transition team have that gives them the right to do this job of going to state agencies and gathering information?" I realized that the reporter's attitude was a perfect reflection of the lack of respect for anyone not part of a self-perpetuating political establishment. Well, the qualifications and credentials of our citizens to examine their government are quite simple—they own it. They pay the full freight because before government can do something for us, it must first take something from us. My goal as governor will not be to see how much money we can collect in the state treasury but how we can raise the standard of living of a working family by leaving more in their pockets in the first place.

2. Government should not penalize productivity and subsidize irresponsibility. Welfare that goes to able-bodied adults should be conditioned upon work and should be a temporary hand up instead of a permanent handout. Let's remember that the burdens of teenage pregnancy should not fall only on the mother or the taxpayers. The father should be required to pay for doctor bills, diapers, and putting food on the table.

3. Let's establish policies for the family built on the premise that when given a strong family-friendly culture, mothers and fathers raise better children than governments do.

4. I believe that a good leader never asks of others what one is unwilling to do himself. To put that into practice, I have issued a directive this morning for all of the staff in my office whose decisions affect policy to spend no less than half a day every eight weeks away from their desks and on the job with someone in state government who actually has to carry out the policies. This directive will start *right* here—with *this* governor—and extend to all the areas of the executive branch over which I have control. We will discover that the best solutions to increasing the quality of your government will come from places other than the Capitol.

5. Government should actually welcome the participation of citizens from the private sector. After all, if a government agency is doing all it can to run efficiently, it should be delighted to have others view its performance. A few months ago here in Arkansas, a non-partisan, independent, volunteer, citizens task force was conceived. The Murphy Commission, led by El Dorado businessman Madison Murphy, has signed more than 100 professional and

business leaders from throughout the state who have committed to developing recommendations to streamline state government and make it more accountable. They will seek to examine the role and functions of state government, including its structure and budgeting and spending process. This kind of partnership can create the synergy giving the private sector insight into the complexities of government and the public sector a chance to help solve problems. Earlier today, I issued a directive to our state agencies, instructing them to give the Murphy Commission access and assistance. This commission must be a team effort and present to me, the Legislature, and the people of Arkansas practical ways to give our state the highest quality and most cost-effective government in America. The vast majority of our state employees are dedicated public servants who want to do their jobs more efficiently and know how that can be accomplished. When the commission issues its report, I expect that people in the private sector will realize that most waste in the bureaucracy is the result of outdated and cumbersome systems and not personnel. When the recommendations become law, procedure, and policy we will be able to further reduce spending on the *process* and actually provide more useful service for the *people.*

Furthermore, I have issued today a directive to the Department of Finance and Administration to use cost-benefit analysis on all new programs and to continue the hiring freeze for state jobs. My office is asking every agency and department to carefully review the budget requests to look for every possible cost-saving measure before we begin the process of executive review in the coming weeks. Advocates for each existing program need to demonstrate its effectiveness.

6. I believe that the best government is the most local government. This means we need to welcome the growing decentralization of the federal government as states are empowered to match delivery of government services to actual needs. But as one who is neither afraid of nor resistant to such an effort, I recognize two things: First, it means the governor and the legislature must be willing to accept responsibility for the outcomes of our policies. Second, it means that if we merely centralize the power of government at the state level, we haven't gone far enough. More decisions made by county and city leaders, and by local employees of state government is the right way to go.

7. In education, we have succeeded in placing computers in many of our classrooms, but cannot ignore the need for building character. Knowledge of facts without the wisdom to use those facts for good is like having a computer loaded with data but without the operating system necessary to process the data into usable form. Government's involvement in education should be to establish clear and concise standards developed by citizens and educators throughout our state and make certain that the resources of our state are distributed fairly among the students and school districts. We will strive to give a greater share of education decisions to classroom teachers, parents, and locally elected school boards. Government should be above all a resource, not merely a regulator of education. Most important, our schools must provide a safe learning atmosphere with zero tolerance for teenage terrorism.

8. I believe government should facilitate rather than complicate life for those who create jobs by running a business. The philosophy of this governor is that the government has done its

job well when our regulations keep people in business by letting them achieve high standards of service and safety instead of running people out of business with over-reaching rules and regulations that cost jobs and profits.

9. Our tax policies should be fair to those who work hard for their paychecks. Ultimately, we need *comprehensive* tax reform, touching all aspects of how we take money from our citizens. Such an approach should ensure that from income tax to property tax, every Arkansan is treated the same without respect to place, race, or face. One place we can and must start is a responsible, reasonable removal of the sales tax on food. This extremely regressive tax, hitting the lowest-paid working families the hardest, can be eliminated without threatening the future of our children's education, service to our elderly or to the disabled, and without adding unfunded mandates on retailers or threatening city and county budgets. I will be presenting the details of that plan shortly. The broad coalition that supports this tax cut consists of people with a wide variety of political viewpoints.

10. We will prove that when we stop worrying about who gets the credit and focus on what gets done, we can restore the kind of trust in government that has been shattered by the blame-game politics of those who would sacrifice statesmanship for partisanship, principle for personal power, and the next generation for the next election. I have found in my three years in elected office that the overwhelming majority of men and women of the Arkansas General Assembly—both Republicans and Democrats—are honorable people in whom you've placed your trust. You elected them just as you elected me. Cooperation is not optional for us. If we fail to listen to you and refuse to

work with each other, you have the right and even the responsibility to elect someone else to do the job. I am only the governor. There's little I can do without the partnership of the legislature. When you agree with me, don't just tell me; tell them, too. We will then all be reminded of our state motto: *Regnat Populus* ("The People Rule").

As your new governor, I look forward to working with you to close the cracks of past cronyism and to open wide the windows in this Land of Opportunity. You have my word that I will give every ounce of my strength to do my duty so as to honor God and faithfully serve the citizens of this great state.

As we enter into this new era of Arkansas history, I truly feel the prayers and goodwill of fellow Arkansans who, regardless of political affiliation, want me to succeed, not just for my sake, but the sake of our state. I will put Arkansas first, and I ask you to do the same. I will daily seek wisdom from God's Word, and will ask him for guidance to lead our state as governor. Being governor of Arkansas is an honor I could never have imagined as a small boy growing up under modest circumstances. I only wish my father could have lived just four more months to have witnessed this day. But somehow, I can't help but believe he's watching all of it from the best seat in the house. When I was 15 years old, a verse from the New Testament, Philippians 4:13, changed my life. It says, "I can do all things through Christ who strengthens me." I'll do my best. And with my family's support, your prayers, and God's help, I can do this job. Janet joins me in saying, "thanks for your friendship," and may God bless our small, but wonderful state.

Appendix 2

★ ★ ★

Face to Face
and Heart to Heart

These impromptu remarks were delivered to the Arkansas General Assembly after Governor Tucker notified the lieutenant governor and the General Assembly that he had decided not to resign. Almost an hour after he was supposed to have been sworn in as governor, Lieutenant Governor Huckabee and his wife, Janet, entered the House chamber to a thunderous standing ovation, after which he addressed the assembly.

Is something going on here I need to know about?

I think most of you are now aware of the circumstances which have brought us to this particular moment. I want to say how much I appreciate my wife Janet for being with me and for her willingness to stand with me during this very important time.

There was a temptation on my part to simply send a written notification to you, but I felt first of all as a courtesy to you, who had driven from all over the state to be a part of this occasion, because I respect you as elected officials each representing an important part of our state's population, that it would be inappropriate for me to simply send a written response, and instead I chose to come and speak to you face to face and heart to heart.

I am grateful for the response, and I wish that it were this way every time I spoke; but I am going to tell you in all candor that this is not probably an occasion that we want to be here longer than necessary, and I would like for us to perhaps hold applause more so for the honor of the people of our state more than anyone of us as individuals.

I was notified by Governor Jim Guy Tucker at 1:55 this afternoon that he intended to rescind his original decision to resign based on a court motion filed last Friday in Little Rock. Mr. Tucker further indicated his desire to leave the entire matter of his resignation unresolved despite his earlier promise to resign on or before July 15 without qualifications in order that he might act in the best interest of the people of Arkansas.

Ladies and gentlemen of this assembled body, this is a very critical moment in our state's history, and it demands that our response is measured with the only concern being that we as elected officials act with the caliber of calm and courage required for such a moment in our history. I would like to request an immediate meeting with the speaker of the House and the president pro tempore of the Senate so that we can gather in my office. It is my intention to fulfill my promise to speak to the state this afternoon at 5:15 on television. The speech may be a little different, but I will be speaking at 5:15.

I realize again that some of you have driven extraordinary distances, you have given up—for many of you who are legislators—a day away from your livelihood, and I want the public to understand, this being informal time, there is not pay or reimbursement for this. I respect more than I can ever tell you the fact that you have come in good faith to witness what we all expected to witness today.

I look forward to meeting with the speaker and the president pro tempore immediately, and I hope you will be able to hear the remarks that I wish to make to all our citizens, including those of you who have been elected to stand tall in a moment like this and be able to represent not what we think or what we hope or believe; but to represent the heart, mind, and the very essence of the people who put us in these very sacred positions of trust.

Thank you, and may God bless you.

Appendix 3

★ ★ ★

Of Right and Wrong

This speech, completely unscripted and without notes of any kind, was delivered to a statewide television audience at 5:15 P.M. on July 15, 1996. It replaced the previously written and rehearsed speech reproduced in appendix 1.

Good evening, ladies and gentlemen. Tonight I fully expected to address you as the 44th governor of the state of Arkansas. For nearly seven weeks, all of us have anticipated that on or before July 15, our governor would follow through with the promise that he made to the people of our state in late May, when a jury of Arkansas citizens handed down guilty verdicts on two felony counts. The people of Arkansas understood that the governor was acting in the best interest of the people of the state when he chose to step down rather than stay on beyond the period of time which he said would be for an orderly transition.

Tonight I come here with an extraordinary sense of probably the same shock that you have. I had stayed up late over the past several evenings preparing what was going to be a carefully crafted speech. Needless to say, this afternoon that speech went to the wastebasket. Tonight I stand before you with no script, with no written words. Just a few moments to share with you from the depths of my heart as a fellow Arkansas citizen exactly where we are at this very critical moment in our state's history.

It was all of our understanding that today was going to be the day in which the governor's announced resignation would take effect. All of us had acted in that regard, both in Governor Tucker's office as well as in my office and the transition team. We have worked diligently over the past seven weeks, not only in terms of preparing for this moment, but even more so, families have relocated; many people in the governor's office have resigned, taken other positions; others have resigned their work to come to work for me; children have been enrolled in schools; there has been a lot of activity.

But my fellow citizens, let me tell you that this is not about the convenience to anyone. This is far bigger than simple job changes for those of us who have anticipated having to find something or having something find us. What really is at issue tonight is a simple question between right and wrong.

This afternoon I spent a lot of time listening to legal counsel and experienced people of the law. There are as many opinions as there are lawyers, as you know. But as this afternoon and this hour approached, I realized that this is not a time for a committee decision. What we have to do is come to a place where we take clear and decisive action. Because, frankly, that is exactly what you have elected us to do. Let me give you some of the chronology of what has happened today and how we plan to respond to it.

In the first place, just before 2:00, approximately 1:55, I received a telephone call from Governor Tucker indicating to me that he had changed his mind about resigning. Even at this late hour, he indicated that he was drafting and preparing to sign a letter which would simply temporarily give the duties and responsibilities of the governor's office to me in my capacity as lieutenant governor. He further stated that this was based on a motion that he filed in court last Friday feeling that there was a strong possibility that the motion filed in court could, in fact, result in his jury verdict in May being set aside—further indicating that he felt like, if in fact he did resign and then the court set aside the judgment, he would have resigned in advance of what was appropriate and necessary.

Let me be very candid with you. I have tried very diligently to be cooperative and, frankly, to be very quiet about the actions of the past seven weeks. The literally hundreds of appointments, the nearly $58 million spent in state money. I remained silent because I respected the fact that the governor was still the governor until a court said that he was not. I further knew that on or before July 15, just as he had stated, this issue would be over and Arkansas could close this chapter of our past and open a brand new chapter for our future. As a result of that, I believe that it was in the best interest of all our people, Democrats or Republicans, to remain as calm as possible and simply to try to stay the course of preparing to become governor. We never imagined that the governor would make any kind of decision like this. I expressed that to him today.

Further, I expressed that in his announcement of resignation in the last part of May, there were no qualifications that he placed on it. Therefore, to add qualifications at this point seemed very inappropriate. As you probably by now know, the House and the Senate were already assembled to be prepared to watch me take the oath of office. In addition to that, there were people gathered all over the Capitol who were prepared for a ceremony at 3:00. But once again, the issue here is not ceremonies and people's inconveniences—the time they spent driving from Jonesboro, Fayetteville, or Texarkana. The issue is much bigger than that.

Following that session in which we received the governor's letter indicating his refusal to step down from office and merely transfer temporarily the powers of office, I spoke briefly to the House chamber. I was met with an extraordinary sense of warmth and welcome, but more importantly, with the universal support of the members who realize that this is indeed a tragic day for our state, I requested a meeting with Speaker of the House Bobby Hogue and President Pro Tempore of the Senate Stanley Russ. These men are honorable men. I want you to understand that we did not meet as a Republican governor and two Democratic legislators. We met as people who have been charged with the awesome responsibility of making very important decisions.

I know that there are many who will probably say that this is going to be great for the Republicans, isn't it. My friends, this is simply going to be bad for Arkansas. No Republican would ever take pleasure in it, nor should any Democrat be branded with the responsibility of it. The decision that brings us to this crisis was a decision, not of Democrats, not of Republicans, not of the speaker, not of the president pro tempore, or any member elected by you, the people, to serve the Legislature. This was a decision that Mr. Tucker and only Mr. Tucker made. And now this decision will confront the 135 members of the General Assembly and will confront me, who right now stands in the role of acting governor.

Well, I take that seriously. When I swore my oath of office to you, the people of Arkansas, I meant everything I said. Based on my meetings with Speaker Hogue and Senator Russ, the following actions are taking place. I asked Speaker Hogue and Senator Russ to talk with the governor this afternoon. They were dispatched from my office at just about 4:00. They were to give him the message that we would very much sincerely request that he reconsider his earlier decision and instead would offer to me before 5:00 an unqualified letter of resignation. That offer was refused.

We then said that, if he was unwilling to do it before 5:00 to avoid the further humiliation and the further embarrassment to our state over this issue, we would be forced to take the second course of action. The governor has been notified that as of 9:00 in the morning, if we have not received from him a letter of unreserved, unqualified resignation, a proclamation, which is being prepared even as I speak, will be signed and put into motion in the morning. That proclamation will call for an immediate emergency session of the General Assembly. We will ask the members of the Arkansas House and Senate to convene on Wednesday morning at 10:00 A.M. for the purpose of initiating the process of impeachment and, ultimately, the removal from office of Jim Guy Tucker as governor of Arkansas.

My friends, let me tell you that this is one of the most pain-ful decisions that I have ever had to make in my life. I do this with no pleasure. I do this without a sense of what politics may be involved. I do it because I have an awesome responsibility to you—the people who elected me and even the ones who did not —to do what I said I would do and that is to uphold the Consti-tution of this state and of the United States.

When the founding fathers created our system of constitu-tional government, the genius of it was that we could change governments, entire governments, if not governors, without fir-ing one shot, without one drop of blood, without one bomb, without a bullet, without bloodshed whatsoever. We must pre-serve the idea that our government is to be operated in the most honorable way, where we act not in our own best interest nor act in the best interest of our own political careers. We must—the people deserve it, the people demand it—we must act for what is best for our state and for those who have given us the sacred trust of public office. That is why, my friends, that I come to you with this sad news.

I hope the governor will, in fact, reconsider his decision today to withhold the resignation that he promised the people. Going back on one's word is a serious thing. I think that all of us can feel a sense of sadness and not joy, and yet a sense of resolve and, yes, a sense of community that we must and we will stand forth true, clear, and tall in this battle. If there are court chal-lenges, let them come. We are more than ready to face them. If there are challenges of those who like to write columns or make opinions, let them come. We have not been elected to take a poll or to somehow check with opinion writers or to even be threatened by the possibility of legal action. We have been elected to serve you and to represent you.

I want to again say how much I appreciate all of the members of the General Assembly to a person. If there are any exceptions, I have not heard from them yet. But to a person, Democrats, Republicans alike, they have made it very clear that this is no time for us to draw sides. This is a time to draw together. And with Speaker Hogue, Senator Russ, their leadership, their wisdom, their experience, their commitment to joining with me in this unfortunate, unpleasant, painful, yet necessary action, we will show not only the people of Arkansas, we will show the people of America that in this state we still believe in some old-fashioned values, in doing what is right. Whether it is good for us or not, whether it is good for our party or not, we want to do the right thing because we owe the people no less.

Several years ago, I lived in Pine Bluff. A dear friend and mentor of mine was longtime and now the late county judge, Earl Chadick. He was a grand old man. I will never forget Judge Chadick had in his office in the Jefferson County Courthouse a wonderful sign behind his desk. It simply said, "Come let us reason together." That is how good government is supposed to work, and I am going to make sure that everyone of us, who can and will, remember that very thought. We will come. We will reason together.

It is my sincere prayer, and I mean this from the depths of my heart, it is my hope and prayer that Mr. Tucker will in fact have to my desk at 9:00 in the morning a letter of resignation in which there are no qualifications. No ifs, ands, or buts. But if not, we will be fully prepared and will with resolve carry out the only thing that we can carry out, and that is the process of impeachment and then removal from office; and then, hopefully and finally, bring closure to this open and oozing wound. Not to the Democrats but to all of Arkansas.

My thanks to everyone of you as citizens who have been patient today—who came today expecting to be a part of a particular ceremony that perhaps you thought would mark a day in history. Instead, we have marked another kind of day in history. And tomorrow it will be yet another moment of perhaps promise.

But here is what I pledge to you. I will make my share of mistakes. Always have. Always will. That is why I am grateful to God that he is a God who looks at us, and with all He knows about us, still loves us, still forgives, still empowers us to go on. Now there are those who tell me, "Mike, don't make so many quotes from the Bible in your speeches." Well, a word to those who perhaps with good intentions tell me not to reference God or the Bible. The fact is, since my childhood that Book and its Author have been the guiding forces of my life, and it would be much easier for me to give up being governor than it would be to give up taking the counsel that I have had from God and His Word.

Now I very much hope and trust that each one of you Arkansas citizens will let your desires be known to your state representative and state senator. You elected them to represent you, and I believe that these honorable men and women will. Don't think that the Democratic representatives don't feel equally embarrassed. Don't think that they have some agenda here other than what is best for Arkansas. Call them. Let them know tonight and tomorrow your feelings and desires and let us all pray that Governor Tucker will do the right thing for Arkansas, for the Tuckers, and for Arkansas' history.

Thank you for letting me join with you. My wife Janet and I express sincere thanks for your prayers and your concerns and your love. And now, simply let me express to you that we want America to see the best that we are and come to understand that Arkansas is truly a small but a wonderful, wonderful state with wonderful, wonderful people. God bless and good night.

Thirty minutes after this speech was broadcast, Governor Tucker's unconditional letter of resignation was received.

Appendix 4

★ ★ ★

The People's Business

The inaugural address of Governor Mike Huckabee, July 15, 1996, at about 7:00 P.M., five hours after it was originally scheduled and an hour after Governor Tucker's resignation.

As Yogi Berra might say, it seems like *deja vu* all over again! Folks, we have been through an exhausting and intense day, the likes of which perhaps has never happened in the halls of this Capitol. We have also been through a day that, I believe, will forever be remembered as a day in which people set aside everything regarding their political parties and stood together to act in the best interest of the state of Arkansas. Thank you.

Let no one say that today was a Republican victory because it was not. Let no one say that it was Democrat embarrassment because it was not. Let today be remembered as a day on which the people of Arkansas were the winners. All of us who stood together, who stood tall, can go back to our homes, to our families. And every one of you in this General Assembly, all the senators and the representatives, can go back and stand proudly to say that, in a moment which was perhaps as difficult for you as it has ever been serving in this body, you stood and did what you knew in your heart was right. The people of Arkansas, I believe, join me in expressing sincere thanks.

I want especially to single out Speaker Bobby Hogue, Senate President Pro Tempore Stanley Russ, Wayne Wagner, and many other members of the General Assembly, who took initiative, who took leadership positions today to give me a new hope about what's ahead for us as an Arkansas family.

Many have been speculating about what will happen when Mike Huckabee goes in and all the legislators are of the other party. Many have said that there's no way that a Republican governor can successfully work with members of a legislative body which is overwhelmingly of the other party. There have been all kinds of columns written and opinions expressed and views bantered in the halls of this marble building that what was ahead was gridlock, what was ahead would be all kind of heads crashing together. I think if we ever in our lives have done something to give the people of Arkansas a moment of great pride, it is today when we show the people of Arkansas what can and what will happen when we gather in this building to do, not our personal business, not our party's business, but when we gather to do the people's business.

My hat is off to every single Democrat, as well as Republican legislator, today, with a sincere hope that this is simply a sign to the people of our state that when they want to know what kind of working relationship we will have together, let's point them to the 15th of July 1996, and let's say, "That's what we did, and that's what we will, because that's what is right for Arkansas." We all, 135 members of this assembly and your governor, stand clear and are unapologetic for that idea. We must bring good government to the people and today you have proven, as a General Assembly, that very thing.

I thank you. I tell you that the people of Arkansas thank you, and I hope that we'll be able to work like this now and as long as I happen to occupy my chair, which, after today, I realize could come and go at any moment. And as long as you occupy your chairs, I want everyone to understand that this would not have happened had it not been for the unity and for the show of support that I received from the speaker and the president pro tempore and other distinguished members of this body. And gentlemen, I could not be prouder than I am right now to say I serve with you; I serve for the people in the same capacity you do. And as we begin a new day in Arkansas history, a day we really didn't anticipate quite like this, I do so not with a sense of pessimism, but with a genuine, heartfelt sense of optimism.

There is a verse in the New Testament that says, "All things work together for good" [Rom. 8:28]. I've often been reminded that it doesn't say all things are good. Some things aren't, but if we are patient, if we're kind, if we deeply seek out what we believe to be the right thing to do, and stick with it, it is true that all things ultimately work together for good. Today what I think has happened is that amidst all kinds of confusion and all kinds of scattered opinions and tension, the people of Arkansas now can look in on this chamber and the one on the other end of the hall and, I hope, the governor's office as well, and say, "We elected those people to remember us, and they did it; and we're grateful, we're proud, and we want them to show us more." That's how to make Arkansas an even better state—and that's tough to do because it's already the best there is!

Let me express a word that I hope you will understand needs to be said tonight. I for one am grateful, genuinely grateful, that in the last moments, Governor Tucker did in fact choose to do what was best for the state and make the decision to step aside, and to do it without qualification.

I know it was a painful decision for him. I recognize that it was something perhaps none of us, unless we have walked in his shoes, could have understood. All of us would probably want to be bitter, perhaps take offense, maybe even look back with some kind of scathing spirit. But my friends, I don't know what possibly could be gained by that. What had to be done today was done. The result is that we're gathered here, and that you have a new governor, prepared tomorrow to go to work with you and for you.

What we also have is one who did serve admirably. I really hope that in days that will come, we all will be able to remember him for what he did right, and not only circle around him the things which we believe he did wrong. That is to our credit if we do it. It is to our shame if we don't. I ask that we put aside every bit of malice, every bit of hurt or hard feelings, for it has no purpose; it has no place, and it really adds nothing except attention that, frankly, I think today we've proven we not only can live without, but when we do live without, we are able to offer up to the people of our great and wonderful state the kind of government that they can say, "I trust it. I believe in it."

There is a lot of cynicism about government. We all feel it. We all understand it. We all hear about it. This is our opportunity to stand in the way and to face all the criticism and the cynicism, and to say good government is alive and well in Arkansas again. It's not Republican government. It's not Democrat government. It's just good government for the people.

I put my hand forth to each of you today with the sincere desire that you will join me in that kind of spirit and in singular commitment to the people of our state. Let's absolutely surprise them in the coming months, just as all of us have been surprised today. But let's surprise them with what good government can and will be when we decide that we love Arkansas a lot more than we do any label. The labels come and go, but we're Arkansas to the bone. Thank you, and God bless you!

Appendix 5

★ ★ ★

A Vision

for the Future

Governor Huckabee's State of the State Address, January 14, 1997.

Someone gave me a Scripture verse for today and said, "This will be a wonderful verse for you." I was kind of surprised. It was a person who has never been my friend, and I looked it up. It was Psalm 109:8. It says, "Let his days be few, and let another take his office."

Let me say to you that I am honored to be a part of this occasion as we begin our legislative work together. And I know that as we gather, there will be some extraordinary memories for many of you who will begin what will be your last term of office. Others of you are embarking on the beginning of a new career in the Arkansas Legislature. And yesterday, for the very first time in your entire life, you lifted your hand, and you swore to uphold the Constitution of the state and of our federal government and you embarked upon a journey that is extraordinary: the sacred trust of public service.

And Mr. Speaker, Governor Rockefeller, to all of you who are members of the General Assembly, to the distinguished members of the court who are here, to all of the fellow servants of state government, to former Governor Frank White, to a very special lady who is here today, Mrs. Bryan, widow of former House Speaker "Doc" Bryan, I'd like to ask her to stand at this time. We're glad to have you here today. And most importantly for a very special person, my wife Janet, who I think is a remarkable first lady. She doesn't have much of a husband, but she's doing a great job in her position, and I appreciate her more than I'll ever be able to tell you, Janet Huckabee.

I remember the last time I was here was on July 15. I remember that day rather vividly, and I think most of you do as well. But that was a historic day for all of us because it was a day of cooperation and a day in which every one of us came to this chamber and did something that I'm not sure that the people of Arkansas really believed we could and we would do. We put everything aside but Arkansas. We put Arkansas first. That day Arkansas was a state that was proud of its Legislature. I would like to say proud of all of those of us here at the Capitol who just decided that all of our differences were not nearly as important as the common bond of our love for what everyone of us would agree is the greatest state in the United States.

Governor Rockefeller, I sat in the chair you now occupy two years ago. I saw the process firsthand. I also forged some wonderful friendships with members of the Senate, which I had the privilege of serving as presiding officer, as well as members of the House. I sure hope those friendships last.

But all of us who gather here today do so having been given a sacred trust of constituents. Each of you from the House of Representatives represent one percent of the state's population. Each of you in the Senate represent approximately three percent of the state's population. I recognize that every one of your constituents is a constituent of mine.

I think there has been a lot of speculation as to whose agenda or whose program is going to win. I, like you, have read the editorial pages from time to time. I've listened to the commentators speculate on what type of donnybrook they thought we were going to have. But the truth is that I don't think there is going to be such a donnybrook. I think instead each of us and all of us have come with a better idea than coming down here to fight one another, and that's the idea to work with one another. And I want you to clearly understand that I have come to this chamber today prepared to offer my cooperation to join you in focusing not upon a governor's agenda or a governor's program but upon an Arkansas first program.

I'd like for all of us, and I pledge to be the first to sign up, to put people ahead of party, ahead of projects and programs. That we would come to the place where we would be more interested in trust than we are in turf, leadership instead of logjams, servanthood, not our own sovereignty.

I was out campaigning for Amendment 1 with Senator Mike Beebe, all across Arkansas, and then up and down the Arkansas River as Janet and I campaigned for Amendment 2. Both are amendments I'm proud this Legislature was willing to put on the

ballot and place before the people of Arkansas—and exception-
ally proud that the people of Arkansas chose to trust you in placing those issues on the ballot and passing both of them. They
will save our schools from forced consolidation and court control, and invest in the natural resources of the most beautiful
state anywhere so that we can continue to enjoy hunting and
fishing and the wonderful things God has given us in this state.
But in both of those endeavors I've come to be rekindled in my
deep conviction that the people of Arkansas, above everything
else, are good people. We can trust them. And now we need to
make sure that they can trust us.

To put Arkansas first, we need to not only have a vision but
a vehicle to get to that vision. I would hope that the results of
our efforts here together could launch forth in seeing that
Arkansas could truly be first. And that one day in this nation
that it can be said of Arkansas that we have the highest percentage of permanent marriages and the lowest divorce rate. That we
have the highest percentage of law-abiding citizens and the lowest crime rate. That we would have the highest literacy rate and
the lowest school dropout rate. Let it be said of Arkansas that we
have the highest percentage of people employed and the lowest
percentage of people who are unemployed. That the best acci-
dent-free workplace is in Arkansas and the lowest workers' com-
pensation claims are here. I want Arkansas to be first in highest
moral standards among its youth and have the lowest unwed
mothers rate in the nation. I hope we'll have the highest healthy
newborn rate and the lowest infant mortality rate. The highest
home ownership rate and the lowest homeless population. The
highest drug-free population and the lowest drug abuse rate.

The highest percentage of on-time payments and the lowest percentage of bankruptcy.

We can't achieve that overnight. And no one expects that even in one assembly where we will gather for the next 60, 70, 80, or—God forbid—90 days that we will accomplish everything that ever needs to be accomplished for the people of our state. But I can't help but believe we can make the beginnings of a great future for Arkansas citizens as they look to us for the leadership that they entrusted to us with their votes. . . .

I want to put Arkansas first in four specific areas that I would like to outline: responsibility, relief, resources, and reconciliation. If Arkansas is going to be the great state that it can be and must be, we must put Arkansas first in underscoring responsibility. I believe we focus so many times only on revenues. Today I'll offer a new paradigm of government, suggesting that maybe we've misplaced priorities, believing that what we do with the cash is more important than what we do with character. Let me be blunt and say that all the problems we face in our society are not monetary. Quite a few are moral.

We're going to be criticized for even suggesting that is really the core of the problem. But my friends, I'd rather be criticized for being honest with the real problems than for ignoring them. And I submit to you today that falling test scores, illegitimacy, drug and alcohol dependence, crime, and domestic violence are really symptoms of a crisis of integrity far more than just a crisis of cash. If all we come here to do is to rearrange money and move money from one program to another program, or to spend more money to create new programs, and we never address beyond the symptoms and go to the core of what it is that costs us so much, we will not have been honest with the problems or with the people whose lives are being destroyed by it. Let me illustrate.

Our rate of illegitimacy in Arkansas is too high. The fact is that 88 percent of the women who have a child out of wedlock and never finish high school will end up in poverty. And we will end up paying for them in welfare benefits. Interestingly enough, only 8 percent of women who finish high school, get married, and have a baby after the age of 20 will ever be in poverty. It seems to me that if we want a 92 percent success rate in dealing with some of the problems, let's make sure that our students finish school, let's make sure that they understand the responsibilities of a marriage, and let's make sure that they understand the responsibilities of bringing a child into this world. And that involves dealing with character.

A young male is twice as likely to be involved in criminal activity if he has no father in the home and three times as likely to be involved in criminal activity if he comes from a neighborhood where the majority are single-parent families. It's costly, my friends, when we ignore this issue. Some good news in Arkansas is that in the past decade college enrollment is up 39 percent. That's wonderful news that all of us can celebrate. We can be proud of that. But here's the bad news.

While college enrollment is up 39 percent, our prison population has increased 93 percent in the last decade in Arkansas. Today it takes over $13,000 a year to incarcerate a person in the Arkansas Department of Correction. You realize that for the money that we spend to put someone in prison, we could pay the tuition, room and board and books for any of our public institutions and most all of our private institutions for that same period of time. And if we say that the lack of character doesn't cost us, all we have to do is look at our own numbers in the court population alone. It can cost as much as $40,000 a year to take care of one juvenile who has fallen into delinquency. That's almost twice the per capita income of an Arkansan. Imagine that kind of money just to keep a juvenile locked up rather than to free his life for the kind of salary many Arkansans would envy.

The cost of the state courts in the past decade has risen from $6.2 million to $17.2 million. The more crime we have, the more prison beds we have to create at a cost of about $22,000 per bed—$77 million more in prison expenditures in the past decade. All of that is money that ought to be, could be, should be going for better education, for better highways, for a better atmosphere that we could live in. Sometimes we say we need more money for our colleges, or for our high schools, or for vocational education, or we need more money for immunizations or for child care. The sad thing is that as long as we continue to spend money addressing the symptoms rather than addressing the root cause, we may always be thinking that it's just a matter of money when the truth is that it is also the matter of us taking the leadership and believing that integrity is important and it's got to start somewhere.

I believe that the ultimate role model and leader of life probably is the best source of all for us to take the cue and understand where we need to go. Two thousand years ago, Jesus said: "Seek ye first the kingdom of God and his righteousness and all these things will be added unto you." He was speaking of basic necessities: food, shelter, and clothing. Today, we've almost reversed that and we've said: "Seek first all of these things and character will come along." We've said if we provide people food, clothing, and shelter then they have better character and do better and come out of poverty and all things will be better. We've tried that. It hasn't worked. Government is bigger, our expenditures are greater, and yet every single figure that deals with the social pathologies of the day screams at us saying something isn't quite working.

Welfare has been based on the notion that we just had to move money. And I think now we've come to the realization that Washington has: that it's not moving money, but it's moving people from slavery of dependence to the freedom of independence and the dignity of work. Interestingly enough it was Franklin Delano Roosevelt who said that "welfare is a narcotic, a subtle destroyer of the human spirit." We've got to reform welfare, and that's why we will offer a bill that I believe will give us the opportunity to forever change the direction of welfare to the direction of workfare, giving people a temporary hand up to the workplace rather than a permanent handout to a welfare role. We have for a long time dealt between the haves and have-nots. Now it's time for us to deal with doers and the do-nots, the able-bodied adults who can work. That's why the welfare reform bill that we will introduce will create incentives and requirements to get able-bodied adults into the workforce and take them off welfare roles within two years.

I know that many of you have noticed we've done our very best to hold the line on the increase of spending in state government. It's not altogether been the most comfortable direction in the world. But we've held that line because we believe the government has to show responsibility as well in its spending and that we shouldn't raise our cost more than the people in our Arkansas families are able to raise their expenses, keeping our increases somewhat in line with their increases. I think we also all believe that there is some relief needed to those families. I would like for Arkansas to be first in its position of relief.

One of those things we can relieve them of is the burden of something as simple as getting a car tag. I know that sounds almost comical, and most people kind of grin when you bring up "let's make that car tag thing easier." Everybody grins until they go stand in line at the revenue office for a little while only to find out they missed one of those six or seven pieces of paper and have to start back all over again. We've introduced a bill, carefully researched, and I think you're going to love it. If you don't, your people will. That is to take away that $32 million in lost productivity time from people chasing paper all over town and make the process of getting a car tag as simple in Arkansas as it is in most of the other 49 states, bringing us into the 20th century as it relates to getting a simple tag for an automobile. I hope you'll help us bring that relief to the people of the state.

We have presented over the past several months a three-fold tax relief package: the food tax rebate, income tax reform, and some changes in the way that we do taxing on used cars.

When I was a little kid growing up in Hope, I'll never forget there was a dog food company that moved into the market. And I heard that they were having a sales meeting one day and the sales manager got up and he said, "Guys, who has the most nutritional dog food on the market out there?" And they all screamed back and said, "We do sir!" And he said, "And guys, who has the most innovative marketing program and the most wonderful packaging for its product?" And they all screamed back and said, "We do, sir!" And he said, "And who had the best trained, the most aggressive, and the most competent sales staff in America?" And they screamed back and said, "We do sir!" Then his face fell and he looked out there and said, "Well then how come we're not selling more dog food?" Long silence. Finally a guy pops up in the back and says: "Frankly, sir, the dogs won't eat the dang stuff."

I want to be very honest with you this morning. I think and have thought that the rebate plan for the food tax is a good idea. It's fiscally responsible as well as being responsive to the needs of Arkansas citizens. But I frankly have come to the conclusion that it is about as popular as Newt Gingrich in a meeting of Young Democrats.

I've always believed that a leader is a step in front of the crowd, but a martyr is 10 steps in front of the crowd. I'm interested in leading Arkansas, not being martyred for it. And, Mr. Speaker and members of the General Assembly and Governor Rockefeller, I've got a proposal for you today. I propose to sacrifice my proposal for the food rebate tax plan because I think that when leaders are real leaders they listen and they learn. I tried to do some listening. I hope I've done some learning. And as I've listened to you over the course of the last several weeks, as much as I've tried to twist your arm and talk you into that food tax rebate, you ain't eating the dang stuff.

Frankly, I'm not interested in proposing something that will end up being like a proposed constitution or a highway program, spending all of my energy and time pushing something that will be overwhelmingly rejected. It's not a good use of your time, my time, or the people's money. And I say it's time to drop it and move on to something better.

Now let me tell you what I suggest. I've been listening to some of the proposals that many of you have offered. Frankly, you've got some good ideas. As you know, we have been proposing some changes in the way we do the income tax. Some of those are ideas that many of you originated and promoted. Some of them are ideas that we felt were very good and are a part of our package.

Mr. Speaker, I think you've got a great idea on doubling the standard deduction. We'd like to sign on with you on that one because I think it's a doggone good approach.

We've been talking about indexing the tax brackets for inflation. Tom Courtway has been promoting that and talking about that for a long time. Representative Courtway, we want to join with you. We want to help push for that because those tax brackets haven't been adjusted for inflation since 1971. It's about time we do it now. We hope that the people of Arkansas will agree and give their support to that.

Representative Curran has been proposing a property tax refund for low-income people. It's a good proposal, and it helps working families, particularly the poorest families among us. And by sacrificing the food rebate plan, that is yet another tax relief piece that we can adopt and embrace. Representative Luker has discussed the child care credit. We would like to suggest that perhaps that if we can't go to the 100 percent level that we double it from 10 to 20 percent of the federal credit, making a significant impact upon the people of our state.

Those are the kinds of ideas we can adopt. But there's more to it than just adopting those. You may know we've already proposed taking low-income people off the tax rolls. People under poverty shouldn't be paying income tax. And we join with those of you who have proposed that piece of the income tax package. We would like to repeal some of the recently enacted sales taxes on certain services, eliminate capital gains taxes for homeowners, and increase the credits for dependent children. We think there are a host of things we can do once we take the rebate program off the table. But it's not just about the relief which we can expand. It's about embracing and joining with many of your ideas, with hopes of reaching a consensus, and coming to grips with that early in the session so we can go ahead and get these things enacted and get back home in time for us and the people of Arkansas to enjoy them.

We want to talk about how Arkansas can be first with the resources we do dedicate. I'm convinced, and I think you are too, that one thing people in this state do not want to sacrifice is education. I'm not only the governor, I'm a father and I have two children still in our public schools. And I want our public schools to be schools that any parent in Arkansas can be proud to say: "My kids went, graduated, and did well as a result."

In the morning, our chief fiscal officer and budget people from our office will propose additional money beyond the $52 million in extra money we had already proposed for education. We will also propose, out of those same kinds of resources, to add more money to higher education. We can do that without lifting the budget cap that you and I have agreed upon and worked hard for. And I especially want to thank Representative

George for his efforts as chairman of the Legislative Council for helping us in that budget battle to stay within those lines. Because, Representative George, we wouldn't even be talking about the things I'm discussing today if we had allowed that spending to get out of control. But today, by sacrificing what was a centerpiece of a tax plan, now we have the ability to come back and bring that money to education and to higher education. But let me be very clear. We are going to insist that we not short-circuit workforce development or impede its progress. Because if welfare reform is going to happen, we must absolutely, positively make workforce development a centerpiece of that program. A responsible workforce development program gets people trained so they can go to work with a decent job that pays a decent wage and gives them a future.

We will insist that funds from the educational excellence trust fund, which will be adjusted because of the used car tax proposal, be replaced from other sources so we don't lose those funds.

Ted Mullenix, for a long time you've talked about a rainy day fund. We'd like to join with you in proposing the fiscal responsibility fund to make sure that if Arkansas ever does face another crisis of Medicaid or an education shortfall because of a court case, that there is money there to take care of it without all of us having to rush down here and find new ways of taxing the people of Arkansas unexpectedly.

We'll be proposing tourism development tax incentives because I'm convinced that tourism is one of our greatest economic development potentials in this state. After having made that trip for Amendment 2 and watching the people of Arkansas, most of all watching the scenery we have, I'm convinced that people from across America, if they ever really get a real glimpse of what we have, will come by the tens of thousands to enjoy what we take for granted. Unlike our neighboring states who have dedicated unto themselves revenues from gambling to fund their future, I can't help but believe that our children are going to be much better off when we emphasize work rather than wagering and emphasize the importance of responsibility rather than the irresponsibility of gambling. We invite people to come to Arkansas not to sit out on a big blob of mud where people have thrown concrete, steel, and neon lights together and called it a tourist attraction; but to join us on a float down the Buffalo River or the scene from the top of Mount Magazine or let them see the cotton fields of eastern Arkansas or enjoy a starry night from the clear skies where people like us have grown up and hunted and fished and hiked and camped and loved our state without realizing just what a wonderful treasure God has given us when he gave us Arkansas.

We'll be proposing some education reforms. Senator Russ, who sponsored the original Act 236, will be sponsoring some revisions to 236 to bring more control to the local districts. The state does not need to be regulating 311 school districts. It needs to be facilitating 311 school districts. We need to move our educational bureaucracy from one that rather than being served by the schools is serving the schools, and giving more of the decisions to local superintendents and locally elected school boards.

Representative Marion Ingram will be presenting legislation that will protect our children with some responsible teacher background checks, not some that are intrusive, difficult, and are overbearing, but that are responsible enough to make sure that parents, when they send their children to our schools, know the schools have done an adequate job ensuring that we protect not only our children but our good teachers. We're going to stand behind our teachers and let them know that when they walk into a classroom their safety is important; their integrity will be protected and preserved.

John Brown, senator from Siloam Springs, will be introducing charter school legislation. There will also be legislation introduced to deal with home schools so that when parents exercise that option they are put on the same level as parents who choose one of our public or private schools.

Something about which I am most proud, originally suggested by Representative Ed Thicksten, is a bill that will be sponsored by a number of legislators including Representatives Josetta Wilkins, John Miller and Bobby Newman, and Senators Jean Edwards and Fay Boozman. It is a bill that I think will begin to help us get on track. It is a bill that involves character education. Not indoctrination, but character education. Not that we will force what the students learn. It simply will say that we encourage school districts to implement a program of teaching character. You say: "What are you talking about?" Teach them the simple things that most of us learned when we were at home as toddlers. How to be on time, how to be attentive, how to be respectful. Things like forgiveness, kindness, generosity. Not so much religious values but character values. Character qualities that are hardly arguable but are most needed in our culture today.

In Medicaid, we will propose additional money to insure children. And the elderly are not going to have to wonder whether services will continue. They will. That plan will be presented in the morning in the Joint Budget Committee. I wanted to tell you today about something I think I am probably as excited about as anything I'll ever offer to you as governor. That's a program we're going to call "Kids First." Because if we are going to put Arkansas first, we've got to put our kids first.

Every one of us knows that one in five children in this state has no medical insurance. They are the children of working families in our state. Their parents make too much money to be on Medicaid, and they don't make enough money to be able to afford health insurance that most of us have provided by our employers. We all know it's a problem and a need, but how do we finance it? We will propose a two-year program to coincide with the two years at the beginning of the welfare reform bill. I believe it will work. And if it works, we'll be back here in two years to make it permanent.

The proposal would be to take at least $11 million and invest it in the future of our children. We will add that to the matching federal funds that would be available to provide a basic health care program and medical plan for the children of working families who right now have absolutely no care and have to get it through the extraordinarily expensive cost of going to the emergency room and being treated as a charity case. And for every dollar we spend immunizing a child, we save $10 in the long-term cost of care when that child gets sick.

My friends, I don't think this has anything to do with being male, female, white, black, urban, city, Republican, or Democrat.

It has to do with being responsible servants to the people of Arkansas. I hope you will join with me in bringing forth a program that will make sure that when a child is born in our state, the child of working Arkansans, that child is going to be able to know that some basic kind of medical care will be available. God help us to do it, and God help us if we don't. And I hope that you will join with us in helping to see that it can happen. It can by sacrificing the food rebate and making the shifts we are talking about. The beauty is that we can do that and still hold the line on our budget just like we've been talking about.

Let me conclude by saying that we want Arkansas to be first in reconciliation. I'm going to speak very personally with you for a moment. There is a great need for all of our citizens to be reconciled with one another. Race relations have caused many to be divided. Partisan divisions have caused unnecessary strife. Sometimes it's the battle between those who live in the country and those who live in the city. Sometimes it's the gender battle between the male and the female.

This September will mark the 40th anniversary of an event Arkansas is noted for, and not very kindly. That infamous day in September 1957 when the governor of Arkansas stood at the door of Central High School and said no to the admission of nine young black students.

Mayor Jim Dailey of Little Rock and a group of citizens from this community have asked me to join with them, and I have gladly done so, in declaring 1997 the year of reconciliation in Arkansas. And part of those activities will conclude with the September celebration of 40 years of what we hope are changing attitudes toward one another. And on that day in September, as the Little Rock Nine come back to Central High School, they will not be met by the governor who says "you can't come in" but met by a governor who says "please come in and accept our sincere apologies and give us your forgiveness for ever allowing such a thing to take place among enlightened, supposedly God-fearing people." And let every one of us make it our priority to bring reconciliation. Not so much that we can force it or legislate it—because we can't—but that we begin in each of our own lives. As a part of that, Bill Lewellen will introduce legislation to make church arson a higher crime in this state. I will issue a challenge to churches. Rather than being in the forefront of perpetuating the kind of racism that happened 40 years ago, they should take leadership in opening doors of heartfelt understanding and open communication.

We will not solve all problems. We will not make all people love one another or work with one another or cooperate with one another. I believe that leadership starts with each of us. This year I challenge you and I challenge myself: not so much talk about the family, but commitment to my family and to specific actions that will make it stronger. Not the character of the culture, but my character—that I would every day ask God's forgiveness for my failures from the day before, and ask for His help to be truthful and honest and open with you and with everyone else. That I would not so much talk of marriage the institution, but of my marriage and my relationship with my own wife of 22-1/2 years. That I would show her the respect and the love that she is due. I'm convinced that *we can never legislate above what we practice personally*. We can never ask the citizens around us to live a life that is uniquely distinct from the one we are willing to live.

I challenge every Arkansas citizen to hold us to a higher standard. We must accept the role and responsibility and give them the very best. We will fail them sometimes. I already have. I will again. Let's just be big enough to admit when we do and move forward. Let's be examples, not just exhorters.

I spoke in California about two years ago to a mayor's prayer breakfast in Lodi, and I met a gentleman there that day whom I'll never forget. His name was Dave Carey, and he had been a fighter pilot in Vietnam. Dave Carey had logged 21 combat missions in North Vietnam. In the spring of 1967, he got in his aircraft and took off on a mission like the other 21 he had successfully completed. But on this day he was shot down and captured by North Vietnamese, and put in one of those infamous POW camps where he spent the next 6-1/2 years. He described what that treatment was like and it was just unthinkable—the horrors, the degradation he experienced at the hands of his captors.

Dave Carey told of how they were ready to give up. They didn't think they could survive the tortures. He said there was an officer placed in there with him who also had been shot down. He said he told them three words and encouraged them to repeat them to each other over and over again. He said, "If you'll do this, I think you can hang in there and make it." He said that these three words not only "changed my life but saved my life."

He told how, when one of the prisoners would be taken off and grabbed by the hair and pulled physically down the floor to the end of the row, where he would be beaten to try to extract a confession out of him, the others would quietly whisper as he was pulled by their cells these three words. And on the way back they would repeat these three words. And late at night when one would perhaps be heard sobbing softly at the loss of loved ones or freedom, those three words would be whispered to the cell next door. He said for those many years he was in that camp, what kept him going was repeating those three words. I couldn't help but wonder, *What were those words?* I began to imagine in my mind words like "I love you" or "God bless America," but those weren't the words.

And I said, "Dave, what were those three words?" He said: "You know, I knew that someday our country would come get us and that we wouldn't be there forever. Some of us would surely get out. That officer reminded us that we would go home one day and that we would see our families and our children again. He reminded us that when we returned to our homes, that maybe they could have taken our health, our strength, years from our lives. But he reminded us that there was one thing they could never take from us. Only if we gave it up would we lose it. But it could never be taken, and we could return with it. And that was our honor. The three words were *return with honor.*" May I suggest to you today that as Dave Carey stepped off that airplane, he had accomplished his mission and returned with honor.

I hope that every one of us, when this session has ended after its many days, will go back to our districts, back to our homes, families, and our friends and our workplaces where it can be said that we put aside everything except Arkansas. And we put Arkansas first. We sat down and we discussed and we debated and sometimes we disagreed. But we did the people's business, and we did it with honor. And that it can be said of all 135 members of the General Assembly and all seven constitutional officers that wherever it is we go when the session is completed that we will have returned with honor. We have a great challenge ahead of us and a great state will make sure we get it done. Join me as I join you in making that happen. May God bless you and may God bless Arkansas. Thank you.

DATE DUE
